D0713536

# The
# Laser
# Odyssey

by
## Theodore H. Maiman
Creator of the World's First Laser

*To my father, Abe Maiman.*

*Scientist, scholar, and teacher par excellence.*
*For his inspiration, guidance, and high values.*

Library of Congress Card Catalog Number 00-192140

ISBN 0-97-029270-8

Printed in Canada by Metropolitan Fine Printers
Bound in the United States of America.

First printing October 2000


Book cover concept: Lawrence McCain

Portrait artist: Saeid Mosayebi

Portrait commissioned by Dr. & Mrs. Allen Panahi

Book coordination: Marion Harding

Edited by Pratibha Patel

Book and Jacket design by Graham Mason

Layout by Shirley Olson

Published by Laser Press, Blaine, WA


Visit the website: www.laserinventor.com

# Contents

# Prologue

May 16, 1960 was the day that I succeeded in creating the very first laser. The now familiar dazzling light beam made its debut.

Emerging from that auspicious birth are all the wondrous applications of laser medicine, fiber-optics, CD players, and, much, much more.

While I found pursuit of the elusive first laser immensely exhilarating, my trail was strewn with many obstacles. To reach my goal I found it necessary to defy the conventional wisdom of acclaimed scientists in the field.

But the excitement did not end with the achievement of the first laser. On the contrary, many important aspects of the drama only started at that point.

Since my father Abe, an altruistic scientist, believed that the sole purpose of technology was to benefit mankind and to help make the world a better place, I was not well prepared to face the intricate jungle I was about to enter in the post-laser development period.

In real-world science, intense competition for recognition, credits, and budgets abounds. Perhaps not surprisingly, the reactions from unsuccessful competitors often come out more like political "spin" than science, dirty tricks and all. Intrigue in science may not be what most of us expect, but such is the reality.

I found myself navigating through a maze of landmines. Along the way I encountered colorful characters, and many unusual, even outrageous experiences.

Numerous renditions of the laser's genesis have been written, but without the benefit of first-hand knowledge, writers have missed the mark and omitted key sociological and political undercurrents of the laser's evolution. In this, my first-hand account, I restore the balance and fill in the gaps as I tell how and why the laser really came about.

Hopefully, the reader will enjoy sharing the adventures of my laser odyssey.

# L.A. Man's Light Ray Outshines Sun

## CAL. D...TES SPLIT

### Deathray Hinted in Amazing Invention

**8 STAR LATEST SPORTS**
Complete N. Y. Stocks

VOL. XC · Four Sections Section A · 10 CENTS

LOS ANGELES EVENING
**HERALD EXPRESS**

:1111 So. Broadway, LA. 34 · United Press International · Associated Press · Dow-Jones

Phone PL 8-41M

THURSDAY, JULY 7, 1960 · 10 CENTS SC · NO. 88

**Can Plant 10-Mile-Wide Beam on Moon**

## Light Brighter Than Sun

A beam of light ... powerful that ...

## Hughes Research Victory

# Horror Weapon Looms

Man has achieved a true amplification of light, a feat long sought by scientists throughout the world. The possibilities are enormous and include the horror weapon of science fiction, "the death ray," United Press International reported today.

It was done in the research laboratories of the Hughes Aircraft Co. in Culver City, and was announced in New York today by Dr. Theodore H. Maiman, of Pacific Palisades, who headed the scientific team which did it. Many laboratories have been trying to ... Russian ones.

other qualities. If you could truly amplify it, you could focus it onto incredibly tiny points over incredible distances.

The heat of light amplified to that degree would vaporize anything it was focused upon. The Hughes research established the principle by which this can be done.

Indeed, Maiman spoke of light and heat intensities greater than those emerging from the very center of the sun, and visualized vaporizing parts of bacteria which are so tiny they're visible only under the microscope.

organized by the Hughes company.

The Hughes Light, called a "laser," could be used for communication and to obtain super-clear pictures of objects in space. In many ways, the light resembles radio waves, Hughes said.

The "laser" was demonstrated today in New York by Dr. Theodore H. Maiman, 860 Jacon Wy., Pacific Palisades. The solid-state electronic device is smaller than a tumbler and has an artificial ruby as its heart.

Here is how it works:

1. The ruby is irradiated by an outside light source.

**Turn To Page 6** · Column 3

## Maiman, Inventor Of Laser, Wins Another Coveted Honor

The Oliver E. Buckley Award in Solid Physics was presented to Dr. Theodore H. Maiman by the American Physical Society at a banquet iven in his honor, in New York, last night. Thursday, Jan. 27.

This distinguished award is granted only once a year by the American Physical Society, the highest prestige organization in the United States, if not the world.

THIS IS the third time that Dr. Maiman has been honored, since that day in 1960, when he announced his discovery of the Laser, a feat that was considered "impossible" by some scientists and a hoax by others.

The first one, received in 1962, was the Stuart Ballantine Award of the Franklin Institute. Again last year, he was honored with an award by The Aerospace Electrical Society and The American Astronautical Society.

THE WHAT and how of the Laser has been described, expounded, and written up by so many books, technical papers, company's ...

The light could send a beam of spotlight intensity only 10 miles wide on the moon.

It could illuminate a building in San Francisco from Los Angeles with a beam only 100 feet wide.

From a satellite 1000 miles in the sky, the light could reveal an enemy target only 200 feet wide on the nightside of the earth for photographic purposes.

Dr. Maiman said the light, called LASER from Light Amplification by Stimulated Emission of Radiation

ahead of the prescribed time with a B.S. degree in Physics.

He received his Ph.D. degree at Stanford University for his original research in the accurate measurement of the Helium Lines in the Electromagnetic Spectrum. While at Stanford, he also collaborated with Dr. Lamb, a Nobel prize winner, in writing a thesis on an allied subject.

About one year prior to his discovery of the Laser, he improved and miniaturized the Maser to make it practical and useable.

DR. MAIMAN is now president of Korad, an organization devoted to the develop...

## SCIENTIFIC TOOL MADE FROM LIGHT

### New Device Can in Principle Project Beam for Communication Through Space

A generally held laboratory theory that light could be amplified enormously and then wrought into an amazing scientific and industrial tool, and perhaps a weapon, was translated into reality yesterday.

An announcement by Hughes Aircraft Co. said Dr. Theodore H. Maiman developed the LASER (Light Amplification by Stimulated Emission of Radiation) in a company research project at Culver City.

Dr. Maiman said the device can, in principle:

Project a high intensity light beam to provide communication in space.

Increase enormously the present number of available communications channels.

Focus a light beam that co...

**ATOMIC POWERED**

## Sun-Brilliant Lamp Readied

NEW YORK (UP) — A new atomic lamp that generates a light brighter than the center of the sun was reported today.

Instead of spreading out in all directions like ordinary light, this light sends out parallel beams that drive apart only 200 feet in 1,000 miles, scientists said.

The atomic lamp with a synthetic ruby at its heart was developed by scientists for Hughes Aircraft Co., Culver City, Cal. They claim:

It could fire a beam of spotlight intensity ...

be used to amplify or heighten light picked up by telescopes, as well as generate light on its own, it can help man get more detailed pictures of distant stars.

OR IT CAN be used in surveys of the heavens for specific frequencies of starlight from stars 10 times more distant than those presently observed.

Asked if the atomic radio light could have applications as a death ray, Dr. Theodore H. Maiman of Hughes said it was not pos...

ght so ...ll light ...s wide

...reation

...erent ...radio- the

...n the sun," a Hughes Aircraft Co. entist reported today.

...e is Dr. Theodore H. Maiman, who said a new solid te electronic device, aller than a water tumbler ...d containing a synthetic by at its "heart," is being ...ed at Hughes laboratories ...Culver City to generate the ...herent beam.

CULMINATION OF JOBS

The development at Hughes culminated work done in many of the world's leading laboratories by teams of scientists, some working under defense contracts. However the Hughes' work was financed entirely with the company's own funds.

The light could send a ...e of spotlight intensity ...on the ...ate a ...ancisco ...with a ...wide. ...1000 ...e light ...my tar- ...wide on ...e earth ...urposes. ...he light. ... Light ... stimu- ...radiation ...aves. ra-

**NEW ELECTRONIC DEVICE—'LASER'**
In background is its creator, Dr. Theodore Maiman.

—UPI TELEPHOTO

**FOR THE FIRST TIME IN HISTORY, MAN HAS MADE A 'STAR'!**
We Have 'Moons' in Orbit, But Now Dr. Theodore Maiman of Hughes Research Lab Looks at Heart (Cubed Ruby Crystal) of His 'Coherent Light,' So Powerful It Is Brighter Than the Center of the Sun. (Other Photo on A-3).

# Acknowledgements

I am grateful to many people for helping me and wish to recognize their efforts on my behalf. They include:

First and foremost, my sister, Estelle Kurtzman, for her tenacious support, exhaustive reading of each draft progression, and her continued help and guidance toward communicating my story.

My friend, Jim Cavuoto for his support and advice on the project, and his encouragement to restore my original laser.

Sharon Levin who painstakingly combed the early manuscript to help promote my grammatical integrity.

The host of longtime friends and colleagues who generously and graciously invested their time and distinctive talents to read my drafts and provided booster shots of perceptive insights and sage and constructive critiques. They are:

Mike Barnoski, Tom Wickes, Cecil Gaspar, Bernie and Joan Mintz, Barbara Finke, Ray and Edith Tasker, Lawrence McCain, Jacob Kuriyan and Errol Payne.

Marion Harding for insightful feedback and commentary as well as her prodigious efforts in getting the manuscript into publication form.

My editor, Pratibha Patel for raising provocative questions, which led me to clarify my ideas in writing.

Monica Karamanian for patiently decoding my cryptic longhand writings and converting it into readable text as well as her enthusiastic support.

Thanks to all our loyal friends and colleagues, who travelled far and wide to attend the 40th (Ruby) Anniversary party of the laser.

Above all, I thank my wife, Kathleen, for her phenomenal patience, unrivaled capacity to listen, and unwavering enthusiasm, energy and resourcefulness in aiding in the publication process.

CHAPTER ONE

# Setting the Stage

## The Laser Inroad

The number and varieties of lasers in use today is astonishing. They seem to be everywhere. Their almost endless inroads into such diverse fields as medicine, entertainment, science, industry and the military continue unabated.

Laser technology even permeates the home. A tiny semiconductor laser diode, not unlike a transistor, is the heart of CD and DVD players as well as CD-ROM and DVD drives. As you know, there must be a laser somewhere inside of your laser printer.

The capacity of lasers to dazzle the eyes is legion and is dramatically shown when watching laser light shows or the laser swords brandished in *Star Wars*. The flashing red light at the supermarket checkout scanner and the gleaming spot on the wall that emanates from a laser pointer are reminders of its familiar brilliance.

The major portion of the communications that is received when one talks on the telephone, watches cable TV, or surfs the Internet comes from information flowing through tiny, hair-thin glass fibers. Those *fiber-optic* communications are made possible by the light beam from a pinhead size laser, not unlike the one in CD players, CD-ROMs and DVD drives.

Many medical procedures have been virtually revolutionized by laser technology with applications running from nearly bloodless surgery to exotic cancer cures.

Ophthalmology uses lasers for treating cataracts, glaucoma and retinal problems. A more recent development is getting eyes reshaped by laser, allowing many to throw away their eyeglasses.

Cosmetic procedures have been transformed by the use of lasers to remove wrinkles and moles, as well as unwanted hair and tattoos. They are even used to whiten teeth.

Industry also makes good use of lasers. They cut steel in automobile manufacturing, do precision machining of exotic materials in aerospace fabrication, and are utilized extensively in semiconductor and electronic component production. They even cut cloth for the garment industry.

Modern aircraft, such as the commercial Boeing 767, use a laser gyroscope for navigation.

In the military, lasers are used in range finders (optical RADAR) to provide precise distance measurement to a target and, for weapon guidance, so-called smart bombs and missiles.

Practical lasers come in a variety of shapes, sizes, forms and beam characteristics. Depending on their particular application, they vary from the large powerful multi-kilowatt (1000-watt) variety used in industry to precise carefully controlled beams used in eye surgery to those miniature lasers used in fiber-optics, CD and DVD players.

## Discovery

I am frequently asked just how it was that I discovered the laser. Many assume that the concept evolved from some sudden, inspirational thought. It didn't happen that way.

It is dramatic and exciting, to have a scientific discovery emerge from a dream or a vision that comes out of nowhere, but it seldom does. In reality, almost all scientific discoveries come from building on other, prior, scientific developments.

This was so when the Wright Brothers first worked with gliders, which they did not invent, but did improve upon. They used a propeller invented by Leonardo da Vinci, elaborated on the prevailing status of aerodynamics and developed, a lightweight engine. By combining the results of that progression, they were able to create an airplane design that led to the first manned flight.

Even the so-called *accidental* discoveries such as plastic or penicillin came into practical usage only because their discoverers had the knowledge and foresight to appreciate what they were seeing and, its importance. They had the creativity to take what they saw and bring it to value. *Discovery favors the prepared mind!*

So it was with the laser. It was Albert Einstein in 1916 who laid the foundation and conceived the basic underlying principles on which lasers are based. He formulated and explained the relations that govern the way that atoms and molecules absorb and emit radiation. He introduced a concept key to laser operation, that of *stimulated emission of radiation*. That is where the *ser* in la*ser* comes from.

Then, in the 1920's, physicists C.H. Füchtbauer and Rudolph Ladenburg added formulations that used the Einstein theory to go further, and tie the absorption of light in a material medium, to the fundamental properties of its constituent atoms. But it was Russian physicist A.V. Fabricant, who first had the vision to propose the concept of a laser in 1940.

More proposals and advances in technology through the intervening years served to build a bridge to the laser. My own prior technological experiences, training, and education helped me obtain the tools I needed to unlock the door to the first laser.

## Coherence

When a radio or television transmitter sends its signal out, essentially, all the radiation is concentrated into one precise frequency, represented by a particular station number on the dial or a specific television channel. All of the waves emanating from that radio or television transmitter are in step with each other. And, the emissions from these sources can readily be beamed into a particular direction, or focused to a confined area. These well-harnessed radiations are said to be *coherent*.

By contrast, the sun, electric light bulbs and fluorescent lamps are familiar examples of *incoherent* sources. Their radiation travels out in all directions, as when a room fills with light when an electric light bulb is turned on. The waves that emanate from these incoherent sources are *not* in step with each other and they emit their energy over a broad range, with all of the colors of the rainbow at once, appearing to the eye as white light.

The advent of the laser was heralded as a scientific breakthrough. Unlike the sun and other *incoherent* light sources, the laser produces light of one precise color. Its waves are emitted in phase (in step) with each other. And, its radiation can be efficiently focused to a fine precise spot. In short, the laser produces *coherent light*, with the properties we were already used to with radio, television, and microwave sources.

Incoherent light sources do, of course, fulfill very important functions in our lives. They provide warmth and light, to navigate and read by. However, applications that demand single-frequency controllable radiation such as communications and precision focusing are not easily accessible with these incoherent sources.

By considering some basic physical concepts, the significance of coherent light, the implications of the scientific breakthrough and, the rich application potential that it unleashed are better understood.

The electric power available from the wall socket in your house; AM radio; high frequencies (VHF) used for television and FM radio; microwaves used for communication links, RADAR, satellite communication, and microwave ovens; Infrared; visible light and ultraviolet all have a common connection. They are all part of a phenomenon known as the *electromagnetic spectrum.* These radiations all travel (propagate their energy) at the speed of light. Visible light is a special part of that spectrum since we humans have built in sensors sensitive to that spectrum piece; our eyes.

The difference between the various parts of this spectrum have to do with their *frequency.* The electric power in homes and factories functions at a frequency of 50 or 60 hertz, depending on which country you are in. Simply put, this means that the current changes or pulsates, 50 or 60 times per second.

The enormity of the electromagnetic spectrum can be appreciated when you consider that microwaves fluctuate at 10 *billion* times per second while visible light waves pulsate at about *five hundred trillion* times per second; x-rays and gamma rays are even higher in the spectrum!

The term *radiation* is often loosely used by the media in a negative context. Generally they are referring to the high parts of the electromagnetic spectrum, namely the ultraviolet, X-Rays and gamma rays.[1] These high frequency radiations are indeed harmful to humans. However, in the lower parts of the spectrum, up through visible light, radiations are not generally harmful unless they are misused.

## Soar Higher

By the late 1950's, technology to generate coherent, controllable, single-channel energy only went as high as microwaves. We scientists were motivated to push the frontier of that *coherent* electromagnetic spectrum upward and soar higher.

*Why?*

There are a number of answers to that question. One response is that man just wants to go higher, to go where we have not gone before, just as we keep trying to make higher-speed aircraft, trains and autos. We want to experience and explore the unknown.

A more specific answer: as we move through the information age, we thirst for more and more. We want to have more channels on our cable TV or satellite receiver; we want more telephone connections across the oceans, we want to send more data and have it go at faster speeds.

As the flow of information is increased, the information "highways" become jammed. We need broader highways and more of them.

Progression to higher frequencies makes possible proportionate *increases* in information bandwidth and at the same time, proportionate *decreases* in the size of the "pipes" needed to carry this information. Optical fibers used to carry light-based communications are merely the width of a human hair! Just these communications considerations alone would be good reason to go to higher frequencies.

*There's more:*

## Concentration

The higher we go in the spectrum, that is, the higher the frequency of the electromagnetic radiation, the proportionally smaller the spot that we can focus it to. The same energy focused to a smaller size is more concentrated. This ability to more highly concentrate energy opens up many new application possibilities.

---

[1] Also to nuclear particle radiation, which is *not* part of the electromagnetic spectrum.

Consider, if we double the frequency of electromagnetic radiation we can halve the focal spot dimension and hence, *quadruple* the concentration! This is a consequence of the fact that the area of the spot is proportional to the *square* of the dimension.

The effect of concentration can be appreciated by a simple analogy: If a woman walks across a hardwood floor with flat heels, nothing happens to the floor. However if the same woman walks across that hardwood floor in spike heels, the floor is gouged. The weight in the second case was *concentrated* into the small area of that spiked heel.

## The Leap of Ten Thousand

As noted above, before the laser, the highest attainable frequency of *coherent* radiation lay in the microwave portion of the electromagnetic spectrum.

*When scientists started to speculate about the possibility of making coherent radiation at light wavelengths, they were suggesting a jump from the then attainable coherent spectrum by a factor of more than 10,000!*

Familiar speed records for automobiles, boats and aircraft historically increase at a slow rate. That is the way it is with scientific frontiers too, which normally also increase slowly.

The suggested 10,000 times move would literally be accomplished in one gigantic *quantum leap*. This was an incredible concept and it was hard for many scientists to accept even in principle. Some scientists believed that we could get there *someday*, but certainly not in a single step. Others were skeptical that it could be accomplished at all.

This was an exciting period of time. Could we really bypass the steady slow progression of the past and, jump ahead so dramatically?

If you were to construct a chart that plots the progression of the high point of the attainable coherent spectrum at any place in time, you would find that connecting the points produces a remarkable straight line. Except for the point representing the laser, it is way off the line. According to this chart, the laser was not slated to be here until about now, in the year 2000.

*The laser was created in 1960, 40 years ahead of itself!*

Going through this 10,000 times leap is loosely analogous to penetrating the sound barrier. About halfway between microwaves and light waves, there are important changes in the physics which describes the behavior of the radiation in that part of the spectrum. Devices that utilize the spectrum beyond that *halfway* point take on a significantly different design.[2] The consequence is that in effect, there is a *quantum barrier*. As was the case with the sound barrier, some scientists said it couldn't be penetrated.

## Motivation

What was my motivation in working on the development of the laser? Was it to make CD players possible? Was it for use in fiber-optic communications, industrial machining applications, or for use in medicine? Or, was it to strive for that elusive scientific breakthrough?

In a sense, I was striving for all of the above.

To understand the excitement of my interest in the prospect of coherent light, consider the following: since higher frequencies provide higher information bandwidth, jumping up in frequency by a factor of 10,000 could have enormous consequences with respect to modern communications. That is exactly what we see now. The fiber-optic cable that spans both major oceans does indeed carry thousands of times as many telephone conversations, television signals and data flow compared to the old copper cables that they replaced.

The proposed 10,000 times jump in frequency would result in a consequent 10,000 times reduction in minimum achievable focal size. *Therefore, in principle, the energy from a coherent light source (laser) could be focused to a dot with an area more than 100 million times smaller than that from a microwave source!* (Reminder: the *area* changes with the square of the dimension.)

One of the very important features of a laser is, indeed, this ability to *concentrate* energy into a microscopic area. In laser surgery, for example, the total amount of power used might be as little as 5 watts or so, the same power level as a night light.

But, that 5 watts of laser power can be focused to a point the size of a single biological cell. The result is the very effective optical scalpel used today in medicine.

By contrast, the energy from the 5-watt incandescent bulb is spread out incoherently in all directions.

---

[2] Just as supersonic aircraft are designed quite differently than subsonic craft.

The enormous intensity[3] of high power lasers makes them capable of piercing almost anything: steel, exotic alloys, ceramics and even the hardest known material, diamond.

Some lasers can also be highly compressed in the time domain and, squeezed into a time slot (a pulse) of only billionths of a second, or even less.

A very dramatic example of this extreme concentration of the energy capability of lasers, is demonstrated when a high-power short pulse laser, is focused by a lens to a point in the middle of the air in a normal room. The air molecules are *torn apart* and ionized. The result is a loud, brilliant, lightning-like fireball!

The prospect of working on a project that could conceivably breakthrough a scientific barrier of such important consequence was compelling in, and of itself. Add to that, the excitement and, competitive interest growing in the scientific community, to accomplish this goal in the midst of the controversy, created by scientists who doubted that success was possible at all.

Adventures have been a mainstay of my being from an early age on. The thought and challenge of entering such an exciting competition, promised an adventure that I could not possibly resist.

Working on the creation of the first laser had additional incentives beyond the scientific breakthrough. In all probability, success would lead to many practical applications.

Sure enough, the laser turned out to be an unusual example of a purely scientific breakthrough, that had enormous practical significance as well. It evolved into a multi-billion dollar industry.

Surprisingly, the laser has not only realized all of the early envisioned applications, but also went far beyond those that scientists including myself had ever imagined.

I wonder if the Wright brothers visualized the Boeing 747 or super-sonic aircraft?

---

[3] power divided by area

CHAPTER 2

# Stepping Stones

## Early Experiences

People often ask me about my early years, perhaps to answer questions about what led me from that time to my scientific career. Although I was not a child prodigy, nor did I nerd like, spend countless hours concocting demonic potions. It does appear that many elements of my childhood were the "stepping-stones" that led almost naturally in the direction of the laser.

My childhood in Denver, Colorado was old fashioned and traditional, complete with extended family and neighborhood friendships. During my grade school years, my parents, my sister Estelle and I lived in the center unit of a triplex owned by my grandparents (maternal) in an older side of town. My grandparents, along with my mother's three sisters Bertha, Esther and Dorothy, lived in one of the end units. My mother's brother (uncle Dave), his wife Ada and cousins Phyllis and Louise lived in the unit on the other side.

As a child and young boy, I would describe myself as curious, adventuresome and sometimes creative. I was markedly hyperactive and had a tremendous reserve of nervous energy. As with most hyperactives I was skinny, some 10 to 15 pounds underweight.

My high energy level often transformed itself into restless, sometimes mischievous, and now and then downright exasperating behavior. There's no doubt in my mind that, had Ritalin been available, I would have been a top candidate.

## Prophetic Beginning

Early in my youth, I developed a "doubting Thomas" personality. I was not easily convinced when presented with facts unless I could get some kind of confirmation. Accordingly, I embarked on my first *science research* project when I was about three and a half years old. Prophetically, it was an experiment with light—albeit *incoherent* light.

I told my mother that I didn't think the refrigerator light was turning off when the door was closed. She, however, was satisfied that the light switch was functioning properly. In order to settle the matter, I crawled inside the refrigerator. My mother agreed to shut the door behind me. *I was right*—the switch was defective.

That episode didn't exactly launch my career, but it was descriptive of my way of thinking that persisted through the years. In fact, as my story unfolds it will become apparent that my wary outlook invited me to question and challenge, the status quo. I was motivated to explore further, when others were content to accept what seemed to be obvious.

## Early Adventures

Although most youngsters are curious and adventuresome, I frequently pushed the envelope and probably got into more trouble than most.

When I was around four and a half years old, during a delivery, the laundry man left his truck in the driveway with the motor running.[4] That active truck mesmerized me. I climbed in, explored the controls and managed to get the transmission in reverse gear. I gave it some gas and rammed the truck onto the curb across the street before it came to a stop. I was quite shaken up but exhilarated by the adventure. Luckily, I didn't hit anyone; the only casualty was a damaged truck.

A few years later, I became curious about the operation of the clothes wringer on our washing machine. *I experimented.* I held onto a shirt to see what would happen as it progressed into the rollers. I found the answer: before I knew it, my arm (literally) was stuck in the wringer

---

[4] It was quite normal to have groceries, laundry, milk and ice delivered to the house during that time period.

up to my elbow. I panicked, but again I was lucky; the machine jammed and I escaped without real physical harm. It was another traumatic learning experience.

Looking back, I'm surprised that I escaped my dangerous exploits without broken bones.

Another interest. I had a fascinating curiosity with the magic of chemicals. To me, the array of cosmetics my aunts Bertha and Esther kept in my grandmother's bathroom next door was a chemical laboratory. When no one was around, I mixed a little bit of this with a little bit of that to see what would happen. I found out! My aunts became downright unfriendly.

Even on the rare occasion that I was blameless, I seemed to have a knack for getting into trouble. One day, while playing softball on the vacant lot next to my grandmother's house, I was up at bat. Without warning, a neighbor holding my two-year old sister in her arms came up behind me. As I swung backwards in preparation for an attempted hit, Estelle was struck in the forehead. I was blamed, my grandmother took my bat and hid it.

Estelle survived fine without brain damage. I know this because in subsequent years, she consistently got better scores on IQ tests than I did and, she is plenty bright and sassy today.

Since I kept getting into hot water with my parents and older relatives, I was constantly being reprimanded and punished. I was certain my parents and family didn't understand me. I looked for a way to escape. One day it looked like the right opportunity had come.

The iceman—*there really was an iceman*—was delivering ice for my grandmother's icebox. I climbed into the back of his truck without him detecting me. Alas, as he proceeded down the street, into the next block, a neighbor spotted me in the back of the truck. My getaway was aborted.

## Games and books

As a boy, my friends and I played the usual games of that period. Without the benefit of computer games to challenge us, we devised our own entertainment. For example, there was "cops and robbers". We designed and made our own guns out of wood. The ammunition was a heavy-duty rubber band cut from an old automobile tire inner tube. The top of the band was secured with a clothespin, which, in turn, acted as the trigger. A hit from one of those guns was not pleasant. Of course we also played with the more innocuous water pistols.

We also didn't have access to the array of exotic plastic toys of today. Instead, we became obsessed with creative ways to utilize tin cans such as "kick the can". I don't remember the rules, but the object was indeed to do just that. Naturally, I was more interested in a more dangerous version of the pastime of dealing with the cans. My friends and I would put a lighted firecracker under an inverted empty soup can and then watch, as it soared 15 or 20 feet into the air. Since frisbees weren't invented, we used the tops of coffee cans to play catch. I have a permanent scar on my forehead to remind me of that activity.

As a book reader my interests were narrowly directed toward adventure stories. I was fascinated with the *Adventures of Tom Sawyer and Huckleberry Finn*. I must have read the *Adventures of Robin Hood* as well as Zane Grey's *The Lone Star Ranger* five times or more. *Paul Bunyan* and *Gulliver's Travels* were also favorites in my personal library.

I read some of Edgar Allen Poe's works and remember being frightened of the dark for years after I read *The Murders in Rue Morgue*. I kept imagining that the murderous orangutan from Poe's story was crawling into my window.

My father kept nagging me to read Jules Verne's *20,000 Leagues Under the Sea* and I finally did. No doubt about it, the creative, futuristic mind of Verne was remarkable. But I was not nearly as enthralled by Verne's writing style as I was by the authors noted above.

I was captivated by Albert Payson Terhune's glorified adventure stories about collie dogs. I read every one of Terhune's books and became obsessed with the virtues of collies. Consequently, I couldn't have been more excited and happy than, when my aunt Bertha presented me with a collie for my 11th birthday.

Princie was indeed a very special dog and a great companion. If dogs can have a personality, Princie had it. He completely lived up to the exalted pedestal Terhune carved out for collies in his books ... and more.

### School antics

You have probably guessed by now that I may have had problems coping with the structure of a public school system. My restless and mischievous ways consistently got me into difficulty. I was either called down for talking, or generally disrupting the class and I spent a lot of time in the corner, often with a "dunce cap".

One day, my sixth grade teacher left the room briefly to confer with another teacher. She returned to find the class into wild disarray; we were throwing paper airplanes and generally, having a great and loud time. My teacher had no trouble discerning that I was responsible for the uproar. She said, "Well, there is one thing about Theodore, it doesn't matter whether he's working on a math problem or raising the roof— *he puts his whole heart and soul into it.*"

There was only one grade-school teacher, Mrs. Nettleton, who effectively channeled my restless misbehavior. Quite simply, she gave me special assignments. It worked; I never did get into trouble in Mrs. Nettleton's class.

Obviously, the three "R's" didn't resonate with me; too much routine and memorization. I didn't start to get interested in school until I encountered algebra and chemistry. I was mesmerized with the *magic* of chemical reactions and challenged by the *puzzles* to solve with equations.

My father had specific plans for my future.[5] He was quite concerned and steered me in other directions when I became captivated with the chemical processes that I worked with at an after high school job. Becoming a chemist was not what he had in mind for my career. He wanted me to be trained in medical electronics.

## Introduction to Electronics

My father Abe was a very inventive electrical engineer. During the major part of his professional career, he worked for several divisions of the American Telephone and Telegraph Company (AT&T) including, the Western Electric Company, The Mountain States Telephone Company (now US West) and Bell Telephone Laboratories.

It was my father who introduced me to the world of technology, and had a very profound and positive influence on my professional interests.

My father always kept a small electronics laboratory, either in the basement or the attic of our home, wherever we lived. It was there that he explored his many creative ideas.

---

[5] To be elaborated on later.

Inspired by my father and his home laboratory, I started to pick up hobby books in the library. I remember one of those books *Fun With Electricity* very well. The book was filled with fascinating experimental projects. I devoured the book and built every project that was listed in it.

To me, my father's home laboratory looked like a fun place to be. I was enchanted with the scientific gadgets that abounded there. One of these was a sophisticated measuring instrument called an oscilloscope. The heart of that instrument was a tiny tube that measured only one inch diagonally, similar to the picture tube in a TV set. The difference is that the oscilloscope tube is used to display pictures of an electronic signal instead of television programs.

I had just completed making a powerful electromagnet by following instructions from my *Fun With Electricity* book. I knew that the oscilloscope picture could be altered and distorted by bringing a magnet near it, so I tried the idea out using my new electromagnet. Sure enough, I was able to produce many interesting shapes on the tube. However, I did not take into account the fact that the shell of this primitive tube was made of a magnetic iron alloy. All of a sudden, the tube jumped out and rammed into my electromagnet. The tube was shattered.

My father was incensed when he discovered that his prize instrument had been broken. He couldn't figure out what happened and I didn't volunteer an explanation. He didn't discover the truth until I owned up to him on his 90th birthday.

Despite this episode, using the equipment available in my father's laboratory, I progressed on to more sophisticated projects like design of audio amplifiers and building primitive radios.

## Abe's Creative Ideas

In his home laboratory, my father invented a device later to be known as the automobile vibrator. This mechanism was able to convert the electrical potential of the 6-volt automobile storage battery to 180 volts direct current needed to operate vacuum tubes in the car radios of the 1930's and 40's. In modern parlance, this may have been the first *DC-to-DC converter.*

His colleagues, who did not have the vision to appreciate the practicability of his device, discouraged him and consequently, my father chose not to pursue his invention. Not too long afterward, the

Motorola Company re-invented his device and for some 20 years there was a vibrator, essentially like the one my father had invented, in every automobile radio.

Abe also developed an electronic stethoscope before anyone took the field of medical electronics seriously. Unfortunately, when he presented a working model of his stethoscope to a cardiologist the response was "yes, I can hear more information coming through, but since I'm not trained to appreciate this I don't know what to do with it."

My father also came up with a number of advances in the design of audio sound systems before the term *hi-fi* came into being. In the midst of working on his amplifier experiments, he had on occasion, wires strewn all over the living room floor. My mother had difficulty navigating through this maze and would often get her feet caught in the wires. Plainly irritated, he told her, "I don't know what your problem is, Princie has no difficulty getting through the wires without mishap." ... In his later years, my father mellowed.

A large part of my father's career was spent in the engineering department of the Mountain States Telephone Company in Denver, Colorado. There he designed and developed the first *dial-by-radio* system, a technological breakthrough. He demonstrated the practicality of his concept by setting up a successful microwave link between Los Alamos and Albuquerque, New Mexico. Interestingly, my father's boss had predicted that my father's idea wouldn't work, that "you will not be able to get the ringing signal through."

I learned some important lessons and, a picture was starting to develop in my head. Authority is not necessarily correct in its assessment of fresh new ideas. From the automobile vibrator experience, I learned that if you embark into the new and unknown, you might not get a consensus from your colleagues—even when you have a valid concept.

### Abe's Values

My father kept close tabs on me. He was tough and demanding, yet at the same time, he was a warm loving father. I always had the feeling that in times of trouble he would come through. Whenever illness struck, he was right there. On one occasion, when I was but a baby, through his fast actions and knowledge of first aid, he saved my life.

Abe and I were very close. We would oft-times play chess together and we had a special bond between us because, we could spend hours discussing his inventive projects in some detail, as well as electronics in general. In that sense, he was probably closer to me than my sister, Estelle, who in turn was much closer and communicative with my mother.

There was very little communication between my mother and me (after our joint refrigerator experiment), except … when she was chasing me around the table screaming at me, "Stop behaving like a clown in class." Unfortunately, my mother suffered from dementia at an early age and at 72 succumbed to Alzheimer's disease.

Although my father didn't take me to ball games, parades, zoos and the like, my uncle Dave, my mother's brother, did happily pick up that banner. I remember going to parades with my cousin Phyllis, the two of us sitting on my uncle's shoulder[6] so that we could get a better view.

I most admired my father for his high-level of integrity and the way he dealt fairly with people. In his value system, possibly somewhat naive, his view of science was purely altruistic. He believed its only purpose was to help mankind and make the world a better place to live in.

### Nollenberger Electric

When I was 12, I got an after school job. I rode my bicycle to a farm 13 miles outside of Denver and signed on to pick strawberries. That lasted one day. There's nothing like the taste of freshly picked fruit right out of the ground; I ate too many strawberries. The next day I went to the farm across the way and picked raspberries. I netted a little more this time but concluded that berry picking was not going to work for me.

I changed direction and focused on the possibility of an "in-town" job. As I searched the Denver downtown area I noticed an electrical appliance repair shop. I approached the owner Mr. Nollenberger and applied for a job repairing appliances. He looked startled at what must have appeared to him a brazen suggestion. He thought a moment and said, "I need someone to help with cleanup, sweep the floor, etc. I'll pay you 25 cents an hour."

It was clear to me that Mr. Nollenberger wasn't about to believe that a 12-year old could be trusted with repair work. I accepted his offer. My thinking was that I would be able to convince him I could handle the repair work when he got to know me better.

---

[6] Uncle Dave was a "big" man.

I had learned enough in my father's home laboratory to know that I was, indeed, up to the job. I was able to worm my way into Nollenberger's trust and he did allow me to do repair work on appliances and radios.[7] I worked at Nollenberger Electric after school and on Saturdays during the school year.

The following summer, Mr. Nollenberger took a job as an electrician in a defense plant. It was the beginning of World War II, a year before the fateful bombing of Pearl Harbor. He asked me and I agreed to run the repair shop on my own. I was 13. Unfortunately, a pay raise was not part of the deal.

The following year, buoyed by my career success, I found another job repairing electrical appliances in downtown Denver. There, I got my 40 percent pay increase, taking me to 35 cents per hour.

By the time I reached high school I had a pretty full schedule. I was taking clarinet lessons and joined the school band. During football season I went to school to report for band practice at seven in the morning. After school I went downtown to my job and came home for dinner. After dinner it was back downtown to the University of Colorado Extension, for a night course in radio theory. I would return home at eleven at night.

## More Electronics

During the heat of World War II, in 1943, my father was transferred from the engineering department at Mountain States Telephone & Telegraph Company in Denver, Colorado, to the Bell Telephone Laboratory at Murray Hill, New Jersey. We moved to Morristown, New Jersey.

I secured a job at a transformer factory in Newark during school vacation. I was hired as a "utility boy." My assignment was to move heavy transformers around the plant. I was now making 60 cents an hour. Moving transformers around was a pretty strenuous job. I applied for a transfer to work on wiring the transformer terminals. This was a much easier job and paid 90 cents per hour. But, I was turned down with the reason: "That's too advanced for a 16 year old." Never mind that the task was trivial compared to the work I had done at Nollenberger Electric, but, there was no persuading the wiring foreman.

---

[7] Helpful was the fact that I had memorized the *RCA Vacuum Tube Handbook.* If I'm motivated enough, I will memorize.

At 17, after graduating from high school, I got a job as a junior engineer at the National Union Radio Company, a vacuum tube manufacturing concern located in Nutley, New Jersey. This is where I first met and worked for G. Edward Hamilton. I designed test equipment for special military vacuum tubes under development and also spent time working on the design of voltage regulated power supplies. As a result, with Ed, I was a co-author of my first technical publication.

Ed Hamilton provided guidance to me and had a profound influence, on my training and future career. He took the opposite attitude of supervisors I had encountered in my previous jobs who had told me I was "too young and couldn't possibly do that." On the contrary, Ed delighted in giving me assignments that challenged my abilities. We became close personal friends for life.

At the same time that I worked for National Union Radio, I studied and passed the examination for a first-class commercial radio-telephone license. When I passed the examination, the license examiner told me that I was the youngest person in the United States to hold such a license. That license is the sole requirement for a position of technical responsibility at a commercial radio station.

In the latter part of my 17th year, I enlisted in the United States Navy. I was accepted into the radar and communications training program called The Captain Eddy Program. My naval radar experience furthered and strengthened my electronics knowledge.

CHAPTER 3

# The Ivory Tower

## Changing Direction

While I was working at National Union Radio, I became intrigued with an unexpected phenomenon in the operation of the special vacuum tubes that were under development at that time. In the dark, we could see an eerie glow emanating from inside the tube. I was frustrated when the tube-design engineers disagreed on the explanation.[8]

That incident made a profound impression on me. I was curious and hungry for a more complete understanding of those phenomena. I realized that a more thorough grounding in physics was required to understand what was going on.

As a result, I decided to broaden the scope of my formal education and study physics, instead of limiting my knowledge to electrical engineering. Subsequently, I did undergraduate course work in both engineering and physics at the University of Colorado (CU) at Boulder and graduated with a Bachelor of Science Degree in Engineering-Physics.

---

[8] One possibility was fluorescence of the tube's glass envelope; another was a background discharge from residual gas in the tube.

## Impressions from the University of Colorado

Looking back, I think we all have some favorite teacher or professor that we fondly remember. One of mine was Professor Hutchinson who had been my father's math professor at CU many years earlier. Professor Hutchinson was an impressive looking man; tall, husky and with a thick shock of white hair. I took a class in advanced calculus from him. Besides having the privilege of being exposed to a personable and excellent teacher, Professor Hutchinson's students were treated to a unique experience. If you came to class five or ten minutes early, you could witness Professor Hutchinson *writing on two adjacent blackboards, one with each hand, simultaneously!* What an incredible display of ambidexterity and mental coordination.

Another memorable experience was a conference with Dean Lester, Dean of the University of Colorado engineering school. When he attended CU, my father had admired Dean Lester and he suggested that it might be very enlightening for me if I could meet the dean. I found Dean Lester to be an especially personable man who agreed to meeting with me in his office where we had a relaxed philosophical discussion. As we spoke, our conversation drifted toward problem solving. He wisely advised, "When you try to solve a problem and run into a brick wall, *don't just quit.*" I noticed a granite paperweight with an octahedron shape on the dean's desk. Symbolically gesturing toward the paperweight to make his point he continued, "Go around the obstacles—if going to the right doesn't work, try the left and if still thwarted go over the top or try tunneling underneath. Maybe, you have to go head-on and drill through." The wisdom of Dean Lester's words made a life long impression on me, *never give up until you have checked every possible alternative. Be creative.*

## The Brief Experience at Columbia Graduate School

Stanford University was my first choice for graduate school and I applied to their Physics Department. They rejected me but I was accepted by my second choice, Columbia University in New York. I do not know why Stanford turned me down but I suspect that it was my overall grade average. I had good grades in science and mathematics, but I did poorly in English and History.

New York City was a shock. The University of Colorado has a huge, beautifully landscaped campus. Columbia University, on the other hand, is located in upper Manhattan, and is by and large, a stiff concrete and steel campus. Some graduate classes in the physics department at Columbia had as many as 300 students. Questions in class were not permitted. One needed to make an appointment with the instructor and ask questions after class.

Instructors of powerful reputation, including Nobel Laureates, were a tremendous attraction to this very famous school. However, the very stature of Columbia's prestigious faculty was problematic.

## Stanford Entry Strategy

After a year of Columbia, I decided to take another crack at admission to the Stanford Physics Department and again, was rejected.

Then, I resorted to another tactic, to appear in person at the Stanford campus for an interview and this time apply to the Electrical Engineering Department. My concept was to try to get into the physics department through the "back door".

I reasoned that: (1) I had a reasonably high chance of being accepted to the Electrical Engineering department because of my strong electronics background; (2) I would be able to take advantage of the fact that the Electrical Engineering Department at Stanford overlapped with the Physics Department in some subjects such as electromagnetic theory and (3) I would be able to take electives in the Physics Department and get acquainted with the Physics faculty. Maybe, this would enable my entry into the physics department.

Also, I needed a minor and Electrical Engineering would be a good choice.

I hitchhiked across country, as I was still in the Naval Reserve, I was able to travel partway via military aircraft as far as my home in Denver. The rest of the way I hitchhiked by automobile.

The strategy worked. I was accepted into the Stanford Electrical Engineering Department and got my Masters of Science in Electrical Engineering, after which I applied for the third time to the Stanford Physics Department. This time I was accepted and I entered their Ph.D. program.

Although Columbia University had the college record at that time for having had the most Nobel Laureates, Stanford was no slouch in that department. At Stanford, it was a privilege to be taught by Felix Bloch, Robert Hofstadter and my thesis professor Willis Lamb. All three, in time, became Nobel Laureates.

## Willis Lamb, Guide and Mentor

After I finished my course work at Stanford, I chose to do my doctoral thesis in experimental physics. I visited with Edward Ginston, one of my professors at the Stanford Microwave Laboratory. He advised me that I could make a good connection with a newly arrived physics Professor, Willis E. Lamb. Lamb was a brilliant theoretical physicist and close friend of Ed Ginston.

Ginston explained that Willis needed a student with electronics and laboratory experience to work with him, to jointly devise and implement experiments that tested Lamb's theories. Ginston speculated that Willis Lamb would one day win a Nobel Prize.

Following Ginston's suggestion, I went to see Professor Lamb. Willis expressed an interest in me, but he also had some reservations. I would be his first student at Stanford. Ironically, Lamb had just come from the faculty at Columbia. He needed someone knowledgeable and comfortable with the ways of laboratory measurements. I fitted that bill but, cautiously, he was only willing to accept me as his graduate student on a conditional basis. I would be on probation for three months.

I excitedly accepted his conditional offer and ... after three weeks, Professor Lamb said, "Let's go for it." Willis Lamb became my thesis professor.

## Living Conditions

On arrival at Stanford, I didn't have any living quarters prearranged, so I enrolled in the dormitory. After two nights, I knew I had to get out of there. The dorm reminded me too much of the crowded navy barracks I had endured a few years earlier.

I scoured the ads in Palo Alto for a room to rent in a private home. I found a real winner. Muriel, the landlady, was a recent widow. She was living with her sister Margaret and their mother in a clean, pleasant looking home. During our first meeting, all three women struck me as being warm, intelligent people. From the beginning, we seemed to hit it off together.

Technically, I was only renting a room but, from time to time, the family invited me to join them for dinner. This worked so well that we agreed to change the arrangement to room and board. They got some extra income and, I got the benefit of home cooked meals.

Basically, we lived as a family. I was taken in to their circle of friends and we went to cultural events together. I became the man of the house with the responsibility of keeping appliances and electronics in repair.

It was a warm, close relationship that I will always remember.

## Ph.D. Thesis Experiment

The thesis assignment that Willis expected me to accomplish was a very difficult experimental measurement. I had to devise a way to measure a small atomic-level displacement appropriately named the *Lamb-Shift*, in an elevated quantum level of the helium atom. My thesis title was: *Microwave-Optical Investigation of the $3^3P$ Fine Structure in Helium.*

I was able to apply my electronics knowledge to my thesis experiment. I used some fairly advanced and rather sophisticated electronics techniques that I had learned earlier. I was comfortable with these methods but Professor Lamb became somewhat nervous. Willis was uncomfortable with methods that were foreign to him, in the sense that they had not been used before in the laboratory of Columbia University's Physics Department. He was worried, that perhaps I didn't know what I was doing and might be getting in over my head. My electronics background was pretty sound and I *did* know what I was doing. The electronics aspect of the experiment worked out fine.

However, the thesis experiment required expertise in a number of other technologies in addition to electronics. These other subject areas were new to me. It was, therefore, important for me to become adept in these other disciplines.

I learned to deal with the vagaries of vacuum systems and how to measure their properties. I learned about glass blowing, electrical discharges and also about electron beam launching methods. And, I learned about various kinds of instrumentation used to measure the properties of light. This new knowledge and expertise proved to be very important and useful in my later decisions and strategy to devise an operable laser.

## Reassessment

Success with my thesis experiment proved to be elusive. The apparatus that I was using for my project was rather complicated and its operation depended upon the use of a continuously running vacuum pump. It was plagued with light leakage, vacuum leaks and contamination problems. These pervasive problems were not only distractions but they hampered my ability to get any meaningful measurements.

After fruitless attempts to make the experiment work, I came up with a proposal for a totally new design with a much simpler configuration. I proposed to make a sealed-off vacuum tube and fill the tube with high-purity helium at low pressure. I would thereby be able to dispense with the vacuum pump. This would be an inherently cleaner system and would give me much greater flexibility in the design details.

Professor Lamb, at first, was reluctant to okay the design. He again expressed concern that he was not aware of anything like that having been done at Columbia. By comparison to the methods in use at Columbia, this was indeed a radical design.

Instead, he offered me a totally different, but simpler experiment as an alternative thesis project. Rather than determining basic para-meters of the helium atom, I would make measurements on excited states of hydrogen atoms. Willis was satisfied that this alternate measurement would still constitute a very worthwhile doctoral thesis.

I was persistent. Even though Professor Lamb was willing to give up on the helium experiment, I was not. This was a risky position for me to take. If I pursued my new design and it failed, I would have wasted perhaps another year.

Willis, from his viewpoint was also concerned about the risk of another year's delay. He had made the first *Lamb-Shift* measurement in hydrogen, (a different measurement than the one he was now proposing for me) at Columbia University in collaboration with R.C. Retherford, one of Willis' graduate students.

Willis, however, had not yet been awarded a Nobel Prize. I suspect that he may have been thinking that the new measurements that I might make would help to ensure the Nobel. Consequently if I wasted my time, he saw it as delay for him also.[9]

I argued that I had almost three years invested in the helium measure-ment and should be entitled to try the new design. I was optimistic that it would solve most, if not all, of the problems encountered with the continuously running vacuum system. Understandably Willis was

---

[9] The contributions that Willis Lamb had already made to fundamental physics were unquestionably Nobel Prize quality. His destiny was clear. He only needed to be a little patient.

concerned about gambling on a radical new design, with some hesitation he agreed to a go-ahead.

## The new design

As I drafted a detailed design for the vacuum tube, my experience from the National Union Radio's vacuum tube division came in handy. I found a craftsman to make the tube and mount the internal parts. It was up to me to do the glass blowing to mount the tube to my vacuum system and to fill it with ultra-pure helium.

I was alone, around midnight, in my laboratory in the Physics Department basement. It was time to seal off the tube. I was feeling tremendous pressure, much of my career was riding on that design. The stress was so great that my hands were shaking. *Not good timing for unsteady hands.* I nearly wrecked the tube while sealing it off. Fortunately, the seal-off was a success.

Professor Lamb reminded me about a property of helium. Although it is a slow process, helium will diffuse through quartz. Using this information, I had a very thin quartz spherical appendage sealed on the tube when it was made. I needed a means of containing the helium that would diffuse through the quartz and I came up with the perfect device: a condom. I fastened the condom over the appendage on the tube with a rubber band and filled the condom, with helium. I used the electrical properties of the tube as its own ion gauge and measured the helium pressure inside of the bulb. When the desired pressure was achieved, I sealed off the spherical appendage.

That part worked fine. So far, so good.

Some days later, Professor Lamb departed Stanford on temporary leave to take a guest lectureship at Harvard University for one quarter, leaving me to my own *designs.*

Before Willis left he assigned a task for me to handle while he was away. He asked me to look after his Mark-7 Jaguar, to keep up the battery and chassis lubrication and, exercise it a bit.

Driving around on that superbly tuned suspension, surrounded by supple leather and hand rubbed burl was an unbelievable delight, this was some chore Willis had assigned me!

Before Professor Lamb returned, I completed my new experimental design. I built and assembled, all the needed apparatus and instrumentation. This equipment was quite sophisticated for that time period.[10]

When I made the first experimental run using the new configuration, I found what appeared to be the resonance signal that I was looking for. It was not very well defined and it was buried, in a lot of background noise. A condition such as this is called *low signal-to-noise ratio.*

But, *could this be the elusive resonance?*

Upon Professor Lamb's return to Stanford, I showed him what I had. He was skeptical. Admittedly, I wasn't so sure myself.

I went back over my design. Then, painstakingly, and systematically, I combed through the entire apparatus. I optimized and tuned up everything I could think of by making appropriate adjustments of all the variable parameters.

The tune-up paid off. The resonance unmistakably showed itself. I was able to get beautiful clear signals, *a high signal-to-noise ratio.*

Professor Lamb and I were very excited.

## Stanford Exodus Barriers

I worked to refine my experiment measurements to get significant quantitative results. I evaluated measurement errors and then started to write my thesis. I asked Professor Lamb for a timetable for the completion of my doctorate for graduation. To my surprise, he argued that it wasn't time yet.

Unfortunately, at this point, Willis and I had arrived at cross purposes. To Willis Lamb, the success of my experiment meant that the apparatus I had designed and built, could be used to do a whole series of experiments. Many new pertinent measurements could be made to check out and confirm his theoretical calculations. He wanted me around.

That was very flattering to be sure, but I was starting to get impatient, I wanted to get into the real world.

---

[10] The design included a servo-tuned, parallel-plate, microwave cavity that was powered by a war surplus magnetron; a Helmholtz coil magnetic field activated by a current regulated power supply and auxiliary square wave modulation coils; a current regulated power supply for the helium excitation tube; a light-pipe coupled photomultiplier tube; a sensitive Q-multiplier tuned low-noise amplifier and a phase detector.

By this time, I had passed my physics department's doctoral written and oral examinations. I had to take the oral examination twice. The first time, one of the examining professors, Marvin Chodorow, noticed that I had gotten a C in Statistical Mechanics. Even though the rest of my grades were quite good, Professor Chodorow persistently asked me question after question on this subject. No doubt about it, it was a weak point for me; I had a very tough time with statistics. Consequently, I failed that first exam. I think Professor Lamb was more embarrassed than I was, but I came through fine the second time around with a different examination committee.

Willis asked me about my language requirements: two are needed for a Ph.D. I informed him that I had passed the German examination, but that I had not yet passed the French examination. He asked me if I knew French at all, I admitted that I did not.

It was my intention to take three weeks off, study, and then, hopefully pass the French examination. A friend of mine had succeeded using this method. To meet the Ph.D. science language requirement, you are not required to *speak* the language; you only need to translate applicable French scientific papers. A dictionary may even be used.

When I revealed my plan, I saw an ominous expression come over Willis' face that worried me. I immediately went into French study mode for a couple of weeks, not providing him with time to object, then went to see the examiner in charge of the Ph.D. French requirement.

He was a charming, old, native Frenchman. As we progressed with the examination, he said, "You appear to be a bit rusty." I admitted that I wasn't rusty, but that I had only recently taught myself French. "Oh, in that case you are doing very well, but perhaps you need to work at it a little more."

I explained that this was the only requirement left for my doctorate.

"You mean, if I don't pass you, I would be holding up your degree?" he asked.

"Right," I said. (It was true).

He asked for my pen and signed off.

About a week later, I again brought up the exit timetable to Professor Lamb. He said, "You don't have French."

"Yes I do," I replied.

Surprised, he confided that he had planned to convince the French examiner to give me a "hard time." Clearly, I had read Willis correctly when I interpreted his facial expression in our prior discussion.

Visibly disappointed, Professor Lamb tried to negotiate with me an expeditious Ph.D. approval if I would agree to stay on as a post-doctoral research fellow for a couple of years. No, I was anxious to get out of that physics basement, into the sunlight.

## Exodus Strategy

Some time in January or February 1955 I visited Professor Lamb in his office and told him that I would need to be finished and out before April 17.

"What?" He was shocked. "Why is that?" he asked. (You don't tell your thesis professor when you're finished; it's the other way around). I said that I had booked a passage on an around-the-world cruise, which set sail on April 17. "You had better cancel and get your money back," he said.

"I can't." I told him. "It's not refundable in the six months prior to sailing."

"Your thesis isn't written," he countered.

"It will be," I responded.

"Your parents will miss out your graduation ceremony in June."

My parents didn't attend my high school graduation because I didn't graduate.[11] They didn't attend the graduation for my Bachelor's degree because it was awarded in the spring of 1949 and the University of Colorado is on the quarter system. They weren't at the ceremony for my Masters (I forgot why). Consequently, Willis' argument didn't get to me.

---

[11] I successfully completed three years of attendance at North High School in Denver, Colorado. During the height of World War II, my father was transferred from The Mountain States Telephone and Telegraph Co. in Denver to the Bell Telephone Laboratories in Murray Hill, New Jersey.

The New Jersey high school that I attended required four years of English credits whereas Denver only demanded three. I had many other extra credits but the school principal was not willing to take these into consideration or my involuntary uprooting from the on-going war. Consequently, I didn't graduate.

I had more than enough high school credits to qualify for admittance to The University of Colorado and was able to pass their entrance exam. A high school diploma was not required.

In November 2000, North High School plans to award me an honorary high school degree.

Professor Lamb had a frustrated look on his face. He didn't talk to me for several days.

I was taking a big chance. If Willis didn't sign off on my thesis, I would have to start all over with another thesis professor.

Ironically, I had put myself in a box. Had I switched to the easier hydrogen measurement as Willis had suggested, I would not have had this problem.

I did a much more difficult experiment and now I couldn't get out because of my success.

### The Plea Bargain

Professor Lamb came up with another deal, a "plea bargain". By now, Willis had a second Ph.D. candidate, Irwin Wieder. Wieder had had little laboratory experience and that, posed a problem. Professor Lamb agreed to "let me go out" if I would teach Irwin the ins-and-outs of my apparatus. Wieder would in turn assist me in making my final measurements. I agreed to the proposal.

As promised, I showed Irv how to operate my apparatus and he helped me get the final data for my thesis experiment. Irv and I got along well and we were able to release some of the tension in the lab with his jokes, he used to call me "Uncle Ted".

Irv was a newlywed and I remember that, from time to time, he would bring his very attractive new spouse to visit our laboratory to view the progress of the experiment. Irv lovingly referred to his wife, as "JP" and I never knew her by any other name.

I finished my thesis, got approval, and was awarded my doctorate. Professor Lamb and I jointly submitted a paper based on my thesis to the journal, *Physical Review*.

### The Laser Connection

On one occasion, during the time that I was Willis Lamb's student, he modestly shared his feelings with me. He said, "Hans Bethe (a renowned theoretical physicist) has more knowledge in his little finger than I (Willis Lamb) have in my whole being." In my opinion, Willis Lamb is truly one of the giants of 20th century theoretical physics; he need not take a back seat to any one, not even Hans Bethe.

The inspirational teachings of Professor Lamb were of inestimable value to my future career. I probably learned more physics from Willis

Lamb than in all my prior course work combined. The knowledge that I gained from my thesis experiment was powerful in providing me with important tools that I needed later for developing the laser.

## Around the World

The long years that I spent on my very tough thesis experiment were emotionally draining. So much so, that by the time I fulfilled all the requirements for my doctorate I became quite depressed. It was hard for me to believe that I really was successful in earning my doctorate. I desperately needed some time to "let down".

On April 17, 1955, I sailed out of San Francisco Harbor, into one of the most memorable adventures of my life. I traveled aboard the President Monroe, a combination passenger and cargo liner which accommodated 100 passengers, all in spacious, outside cabins.

The age range of the ships passengers was from about 50 to 90 ... and me, aged 28. Fortunately for me, the ship's officers were relatively young. The captain was 36, the ship's doctor 35 and the first mate was 28. I enjoyed fraternizing with those officers.

The passengers soon formed cliques. Early into the cruise, while reading a book in the lounge, one of these, a group of doctors, seemed to be observing me. Finally, one of the physicians approached me and asked, "just what kind of doctor are you?"[12] I responded, "I'm a physicist." In a heavy southern US accent, he said, "We just knew that you must be the kind of doctor that is no good to people when they are sick."

I had never before been outside of the United States and it was extremely exciting to traverse the Orient, Indonesia, India and the Middle East. I left the ship at Naples and traveled north by rail through Europe, terminating in London. Another ship, the French liner Flandre, took me from Southampton to New York, from where I flew back to California. The entire trip took about 80 days, just as Jules Verne had said.

The cruise cost was about $3,500. I had saved the fare money by working summers at an electronics firm and also from the Navy contract that sponsored Willis Lamb's research. Unfortunately, the side trips on the cruise took me over budget and I had to borrow $500 from my father so I could get back to California.

---

[12] I had worked long and hard for my doctorate, so I listed myself on the passenger roster as "doctor" Maiman.

It took me about one month into the cruise to "unwind". The second month I was pretty relaxed, and that was the most enjoyable part of the trip. But, after about sixty days I became "antsy". I was ready to go to work and start my career.

## Ph.D. Aftermath

In June 1955, my thesis paper was published in the *Physical Review*.

Irwin Wieder successfully took over my experimental apparatus and quickly finished his own thesis.

In October 1955, I read that Willis Lamb had received the Nobel Prize in Physics.

In 1956, Willis shut down his Stanford laboratory and moved on to take a theoretical chair in physics at Oxford University.

Professor Lamb went on to win honorary doctorates and numerous other high honors.

After I created the first laser, Willis Lamb became interested in analyzing the basic theoretical physics underlying laser operation. In a classic paper, he correctly predicted a physical phenomenon sometimes observed in laser behavior which came to be known as the *"Lamb Dip."*

The irony is: when I worked on my thesis, I was helping Willis Lamb confirm his theories. Now, in a turn around, he was developing theories to more deeply understand my experiments.

CHAPTER 4

# Entering the Real World

## Employment Dilemma

Before I set off on my round-the-world voyage, I lined up a job at a new industrial research laboratory, part of Lockheed Aerospace in Van Nuys, California.

Professor Lamb was shocked when I told him where my first job would be. He expected me to join a university faculty and engage in fundamental research. Willis thought that physicists who worked in industry were prostituting themselves since, at that time, there was a large disparity between industrial pay and university salaries (almost double).

He argued, "If you are obstinate about going into industry, then go to work for the Bell Telephone Laboratories, at least they have a semi-academic culture."

Willis Lamb was very worried with the stigma he might have if one of his students ended up in industry.

An interesting aside: University and college professors often "have their cake and eat it too". They have the prestige and *purity* of being academic professors, but they are permitted to consult for industry and earn very large fees. Their total income can be quite substantial.

My personality and temperament are not especially suited to teaching. I don't have the patience to prepare lectures or to design and grade examinations. I felt that I would not fit well in the academic world. Besides, after having spent some nine years in an academic culture, the last four years of which were in the Stanford Physics *basement,* I was ready for a new environment, one at ground level or above.

### The Lockheed Lesson

On August 1, 1955 I went to work at Lockheed Aerospace as planned. It was a big mistake!

I learned that Lockheed was working on the problems that a space vehicle encounters when it returns to earth at a very high rate of speed and re-enters the atmosphere. Lockheed had a government contract whose mandate was to evaluate and solve these problems. The contract was code named RTV, for Reentry Test Vehicle.

While working on some ideas to make crucial measurements of the re-entry parameters, I started to set up a laboratory and properly equip it.

One of the ideas that I wanted to analyze was the possibility of using an effect that had been an annoying problem for my thesis experiment to make reentry measurements. (The effect is called cyclotron resonance). Another concept was to modulate an *incoherent* light beam to be used as an alternate method of communication.[13]

I never had a chance to work on either scheme. Lockheed had much bigger plans.

Lockheed had bid on a very substantial, $250 million government contract, for the development of the Titan Intercontinental Ballistic Missile (ICBM). The conventional wisdom, at least according to Lockheed, was that they would be the easy winner of that contract.

Then came a very black Monday at Lockheed's Van Nuys laboratory. Not only did Lockheed *not* win the big contract, but also the contract was awarded to the *least* likely winner, (according to Lockheed), Martin Marietta.

The Van Nuys research laboratory began to fall apart. Morale was low and people started to leave. Ernst Krause, Lockheed's director of research, founded a major spin-off called Aeronutronics. This Ford Motor Company new venture pirated employees from the Van Nuys lab, further exacerbating the Lockheed situation.

---

[13] Alexander Graham Bell conceived that one well before me.

I had been enticed to join Lockheed with the promise that I would be working on exciting new research projects. In fact, it turned out that I was just one part of a pool of scientists that was being amassed for the anticipated Titan contract. The project that I had started was shut down so I was stuck spending my time in the Lockheed library.

I felt very frustrated and angry. I had spent many years of my life in university training, preparing myself for what I had envisioned would be an exciting and productive career. I was extremely eager to get started on some important projects and launch that career.

The situation was a mess. Louis Ridenour, an eminent scientist and administrator, was brought in to take charge at Lockheed Research. He immediately put a punitive measure in place in an attempt to stop the exodus of scientists from the lab: anybody caught talking on the phone to Aeronutronics would be fired on the spot.

Ridenour planned to move the Lockheed laboratory to Sunnyvale California, near Stanford. In an attempt to keep me from jumping ship, Louis told me that everything was going to turn out fine. He said: "With Lockheed's money and Stanford's prestige we will be very successful. We have all the Stanford professors lined up with only one holdout, Leonard Schiff." (Schiff was head of the Stanford physics department.)

Ridenour was correct. Lockheed moved up to Sunnyvale, not far from Stanford and within a few years, became the largest United States government defense contractor.

## Marvin Ettinghoff

When I pondered my employment opportunities, a factor in my decision to accept Lockheed's offer was the fact that I wanted to live and work in the Los Angeles area. I had by now started to get connected in the Los Angeles social scene and develop some new friendships. Consequently, it wasn't very appealing to me to follow Lockheed back to northern California.

One of the friendships I developed was with Marvin Ettinghoff, a personable digital design engineer at work. We got along well. We discussed technology and had other mutual interests and outlooks. I was single, and Marv was single again, between marriages numbers two and three. He was very familiar with the L.A. social scene, he knew how to get us into the better parties where we could meet exciting young women. We became close friends and confidants.

The fall of 1955 was squarely in the middle of the McCarthy era. I didn't experience any direct fallout from McCarthy's abusive politics but I observed a very disturbing consequence.

One day Marv got a call from an FBI agent. The agent insisted on a meeting, at which Marv was told that his girlfriend was a "communist sympathizer." He was instructed that he must drop his friend. If not, he would lose his security clearance and consequently, his job. At this time, although there was plenty of work in the Los Angeles aerospace industry, most positions required a security clearance. Marv dropped his girl friend, he retained his security clearance and his job.

## The Irwin Hahn Connection

In December 1955 I attended a meeting of the American Physical Society (APS), held for the first time in Los Angeles. Previous annual APS meetings had always been held in New York City at the end of January. Somebody finally figured out that the combination of New York City and its late January weather were not conducive to good meeting turnout. For example, one year, attendees of the winter APS meeting were unable to get flights out of New York for more than 36 hours because heavy snowfall kept the airport closed and people were piled up sleeping in the hotel lobbies.

At the Los Angeles meeting I ran into Irwin Hahn. I had known Irwin from when I was a graduate student at Stanford and he was a post-doctoral fellow, working for the eminent physicist, later Nobel Laureate, Felix Bloch. Irwin had done very fine work called the *spin-echo* technique, a precursor technology fundamental to MRI (magnetic resonance imaging).

Irwin was a very capable and personable physicist, with a great sense of humor and a very easygoing, fun personality. One of his hobbies was to collect bawdy limericks. He knew many by heart and kept a file of them. At a Stanford Physics Department party, when everybody was in a happy mood, Irwin taught Professor Bloch to play a tune on his (Bloch's) head with a spoon.

When I saw Irwin at the APS meeting, we talked about what had happened at Lockheed.

Irwin was now a professor at the University of California, Berkley but he was also a consultant to industry. He said that he was doing some work for a new department, the Atomic Physics Department, at the Hughes Research Laboratory in Culver City, California. Irwin thought that my background and training would fit in well with the work culture and style of this new Atomic Physics Department.

I followed Irwin's lead and interviewed for a job at Hughes. I was hired and started work one month later, in January 1956.

## The Hughes Cast of Characters

The Hughes Atomic Physics department was conceived, organized and headed by, physicist Harold Lyons. Harold had come to Hughes from the United States National Bureau of Standards (NBS) in Boulder, Colorado. At the Bureau, he had been responsible for developments on the *Atomic Clock*. This is the fundamental time standard used by NBS.

Harold had a creative mind, but he was also very intense, spoke in a whine, and complained a lot. He didn't have much of a sense of humor, I don't ever remember him smiling or laughing. His talkativeness was legion. If you ran into Harold in the corridor, you could be stuck for 30 minutes listening to his monologue. You could always tell when he was coming down the hall because of the sound of his unusual walk.

Harold Lyons was given a substantial budget by Hughes to organize and build his department. He had a good network connected to the universities; he proceeded to hire a batch of new Ph.D. level scientists.

Bela Lengyel was associate head of the Atomic Physics Department. Bela was an impressive physicist trained in Hungary, his native country. He had come to Hughes from Rensselaer Polytechnic Institute and City College of the City of New York, where he had taught mathematics and physics. Bela had impeccable character and integrity. He was the stalwart of the department managers but was organized to the point of being a bit rigid. It was very disturbing to Bela to see some of the new Ph.D. scientists straggle in to work at all hours of the morning after the eight o'clock official starting time. He patrolled the hallways in the morning with a pocket watch in hand and clocked the time each person arrived.

Bela was most annoyed with Leo Levitt who routinely arrived at nine in the morning or later and then, to make up for his tardiness, would leave an hour early. Generally, it wasn't as bad as this since most of those who arrived late stayed and worked very long hours.

The Atomic Physics Department was divided into two sections. George Birnbaum headed the Quantum Physics Section; Robert White headed the Solid State and Cryogenics section. I was assigned to the Quantum Physics section.

George, my direct supervisor, was a friend of Harold Lyons. He had worked with Harold at the National Bureau of Standards; they both came to Hughes at the same time. They were a package, so to speak.

It's a little hard to describe George. He was a bit pompous, with a limited sense of humor and yet somewhat personable. He was very intelligent, at least in the sense of his capability to study and understand physical phenomena. I didn't think that he was particularly creative, but I'm convinced that he was a good student and probably received high grades in school. George was also very competitive and eager to get ahead.

George had a hard time with creative ideas. He could understand and analyze someone's idea but then he would confuse the origin of the idea in his own mind. Sometimes I would present a new concept that I was thinking about to George for discussion. Some days later he would present me with that same concept and start explaining it to me.

"George, I know! That's the idea I discussed with you the other day!"

He would ignore me and continue to feed back to me my own idea as if *he* had just thought it up. This happened a number of times and, on each occasion, was an absolutely jarring experience. I've never had that kind of encounter with anyone else, either before or after George.

Almost all of the scientists that Harold hired in the early days were doctoral level physicists. They included Bob Hellwarth, Leo Levitt, Jim Lotspeich, Mal Stitch, Ray Hoskins and Ken Trigger. Then there was Ricardo Pastor, an extremely talented physical chemist and materials expert. Rick and I worked well together and became lifelong friends.

Of all the members of Harold Lyons' staff, probably the most colorful character was Malcolm L. Stitch. After his graduate work at Columbia University, he had come to Hughes where he was assigned to work on the ammonia-beam maser.

Mal was the bad boy of the department, always getting into some kind of trouble. When Mal talked with you he would remove his false tooth and fondle it as he spoke. He was then on wife number three. The last time I heard from him it was wife number six.

After an altercation with Harold Lyons, Mal transferred to the Hughes Ground Systems Division.

When I succeeded with my ruby laser project, Mal Stitch was assigned to be the liaison for technology transfer from the research laboratory to Ground Systems. He spent countless hours with me as I instructed him on the detailed design parameters and attendant calculations for the ruby laser.

He took copious notes during our meetings. I then found out that Mal had written up those notes and submitted the material to one of the physics journals for publication under his name. I was very angry and reported this information to the management at Hughes. As a consequence, Mal was instructed to stop and desist.

Mal contacted me and requested that we meet for lunch. At lunch he confessed to a further complication about this. The paper he had submitted for publication had already been accepted and was in press. He begged that if he were found out, he would certainly be fired. He pleaded that he had two sets of alimony payments plus child support. I weakened; I let him off the hook ... I shouldn't have.

## A Blind Date

Marvin Ettinghoff, like me, also declined to follow Lockheed to Sunnyvale. He also found another position in the Los Angeles area. We continued to be friends and got together from time to time. One day Marv called to say that he had run into Shirley Rich, a young woman that he knew from the past. He thought that Shirley and I would make a good combination.

Shirley and I met on a blind date that Marv arranged. About three months later, in late summer 1956, we were married. Two years after our marriage, in July 1958, our daughter Sheri was born. Unfortunately, the decision to get married was a hasty one and the relationship was not destined to last.

## Lola

Another interesting (outrageous) character in the Hughes Atomic Physics department was Lola McFeeters, departmental secretary reporting to Harold Lyons. Lola was extremely intelligent and efficient in her job but at the same time quite manipulative. She expected and got various favors from members of the department as a consequence of her implied power as secretary to the boss. (What Lola wants, Lola gets).

Lola, who was unmarried, delighted in flirting with the married scientists in our department. Her flirtation seemed at first harmless enough, but in fact, she was quite a troublemaker. She expertly played on the fears and insecurities of the scientists' wives. At departmental social functions, Lola would manage to have conversations with these spouses. She would mischievously imply to them that she was very close and possibly intimate with their husbands.

Lola was especially successful in stirring up the ire of Ray Hoskins' wife, Barbara, Rick Pastor's wife, Anne and my wife, Shirley. As a consequence, Ray, Rick and I found ourselves, on the defensive "carpet" denying the implied accusations of Lola. She seemed to know of her success and delighted in her shenanigans.

Through the years, Lola didn't lose her touch. She wrote me a letter just two years ago after a very long period of no contact. When Kathleen[14] read the letter she just assumed from the tone that Lola was a former amour of mine.

## Taking Care of Some Unfinished Business

The mandate of the Hughes Atomic Physics Department was to devise ways to push the practical limit of the coherent electromagnetic spectrum higher in frequency (shorter wavelengths).

I thought of an idea to generate higher frequencies using the concept of cyclotron resonance. This phenomenon is the basis of certain large research machines in university physics laboratories. When I worked on my thesis experiment at Stanford, this resonance had cropped up as a problem for me.

In that case, the cyclotron resonance, which produced a very strong but erroneous signal, interfered with the weaker resonance in helium that I was trying to detect and measure. I was able to separate the two resonances, but I promised myself that I would at some later time find a constructive use for the cyclotron resonance.

I submitted an unsolicited proposal, based on my cyclotron resonance idea to the United States Air Force laboratory at Wright Field in Ohio. The proposal was successful and won a contract for Hughes. Under that contract, I was able to demonstrate the viability of my idea with a prototype that used a helium discharge as the working medium.

---

[14] My endearing and loving wife of today.

CHAPTER 5

# The Ruby Maser Distraction

The Hughes Atomic Physics Department had been getting substantial contract research monies from the United States Army Signal Corps at Fort Monmouth, New Jersey. That funding was now being discontinued. In its stead, the Signal Corps offered Hughes a contract to make and deliver a special state-of-the-art microwave amplifier known as a *ruby maser*.[15]

I was selected to head the maser project.

### Reluctance

At first, I balked. Although I had made the decision earlier to work in industry as opposed to academia, I nevertheless expected to concentrate exclusively on research projects. The task before me, to deliver a state-of-the-art *device*, did not appeal to me. It would be more of an engineering project.

There was another reason that I was not keen to work on a maser. I had started to germinate some ideas about the possibility of a laser. My concept so far, was to try to use a solid material for the lasing medium. My thinking was to fabricate the potential laser material into a rod shape.

---

[15] A maser is a device that amplifies microwaves and has some distant properties in common with a laser. That connection will be made clear later in the text.

My knowledge of microwaves and optics gained from the work on my thesis experiments at Stanford allowed me to consider this configuration from two different viewpoints. In microwave thinking it would be called a *dielectric wave-guide*. In optics it's known as a *light pipe*. In any case, I planned to put mirrors on each end of the rod to form a resonator.

Working on the maser would be a distraction and diversion from my incubative thinking about a laser.

I really didn't have too much choice in the matter. Hughes was putting heavy pressure on me. After heated discussions with George Birnbaum, I did agree to take on delivery of a ruby maser to the Signal Corps. However, I insisted on the condition that I would be permitted to develop an advanced model of the maser. I had some new design concepts that I wanted to incorporate, instead of being stuck with the conventional version of that device.

### Irnee D'Haenens

About this time, a University of Southern California student in the Hughes Masters' Program was assigned to work with me as my assistant. His name was Irnee D'Haenens. Irnee didn't have much laboratory experience, but he was eager to learn.

Irnee and I worked well together. There was a lot of joviality and camaraderie between us as well. On the days that we "brown bagged" for lunch, we played chess during the noon hour. Sometimes we ran overtime a bit. Irnee's laid back unflappable manner had a calming effect on me in the sometimes tense atmosphere at Hughes.

Irnee and I were both married to Shirleys. Whereas I had one child, Sheri, Irnee and his wife were busy turning out a larger family, eventually four children and subsequently, 19 grandchildren.

Irnee continued with his schooling and completed his Master's Degree. Several years after the laser development he took leave of absence from Hughes to return to his alma mater, Notre Dame, where he took further graduate work and received his doctorate in physics.

### Standard Maser Design

The standard solid-state maser was a huge unwieldy apparatus. The main component was a very large electromagnet made by Varian Associates. This magnet filled a small room and weighed about 5,000 pounds.

A double Dewar[16] flask was placed in the space between the pole pieces of the magnet, the place where the magnetic field is concentrated.

Inside the outer Dewar was very *cold* liquid nitrogen. Inside the inner Dewar there was *frigid* liquid helium. Helium must be cooled all the way down to at a temperature of 4 degrees Kelvin before it transforms into a liquid. That is only four degrees above absolute zero![17] To dramatize the point, consider that air (both oxygen and nitrogen) is frozen solid at the temperature of liquid helium.

Liquid helium has very low heat capacity, consequently, even small heat leaks will rapidly boil the helium away. The purpose of the outer Dewar flask filled with liquid nitrogen was to provide a cold jacket to reduce the stray heat input to the helium bath. The inner Dewar flask, by itself, did not provide enough insulation.

By now you can appreciate that liquid helium is a thorny material to work with. It is also costly and difficult to make and store. An expensive special refrigerator called a cryostat is used to make liquid helium.

Inside the inner Dewar, immersed in the liquid helium was a microwave cavity. Inside the cavity was a small maser crystal, a tiny man-made ruby about one carat in size. A high frequency microwave generator was used to activate the maser crystal.

The small ruby crystal only occupied about one-tenth the volume of the microwave cavity. This 10 percent filling factor seriously degraded the performance of that maser design. Moreover, it was difficult to attach the small crystal in a stable manner. There aren't too many glues around suitable for liquid helium operation. Instabilities in the maser performance resulted from crystal movements and helium bubbles in the cavity.

This state-of-the-art design was an impractical monster. The magnet was huge and costly; the double Dewar was a complex and expensive structure; and its performance was limited and unstable.

Why would anyone want to make such a monstrosity?

Because a solid-state ruby maser has the capacity to detect and amplify extremely weak microwave signals.

---

[16] "Dewar flask" is the laboratory name for a thermos bottle, named after its inventor, Sir James Dewar.
[17] Zero degrees Kelvin is theoretically the lowest temperature that can be approached but never arrived at. At this temperature, the vibrational motion of all materials would plunge to zero.

## A Radical New Design

I was determined to design and build a more practical ruby maser for delivery to the Signal Corps.

I argued, why put such a monstrous magnet *outside* the double Dewar and microwave cavity assembly? Instead, why not put a very small magnet *inside* the inner Dewar sufficient to deliver the same magnetic field strength to the very small maser crystal? That was the sole reason for the magnetic field anyway.

Immediately the naysayers appeared. My supervisor, George Birnbaum said to me, "You can't put a permanent magnet in a liquid helium bath—it will crack." Well, *It didn't*.

I violated conventional thinking in another way. The standard maser design demanded that the active crystal be attached to one of the walls of the microwave cavity to insure proper operation. Calculations I had made showed that this was not necessarily so.

Instead, my radical design concept was to completely fill the microwave cavity with ruby crystal material. This idea had several potential benefits. First, I could obviate the crystal glue problem and the helium bubbles completely, thereby eliminating the sources of instability. Second, not surprising, filling the cavity with maser material increased the filling factor to 100 percent. The measurement of maser performance (it's called the gain-bandwidth product) would be expected to increase substantially.

When a microwave cavity is completely filled with the high dielectric ruby material, the size of the cavity must shrink to accommodate the dielectric loading and be able to keep the same resonant frequency. In this case I was able to reduce the cavity volume by a factor of 27 times. A beneficial result was a drastic reduction in the pumping power requirement. Of course, it was the tiny cavity that made the use of a small internal permanent magnet practical.

My final design was as follows: I fabricated a ruby crystal into a rectangular block approximately 3mm thick by about 7mm square. My colleague Rick Pastor told me of a special highly conductive silver paint, which I painted and baked on the ruby. The pumping power needed to activate the ruby into *maser-action* was provided by a small klystron.[18]

The magnetic field was easily furnished by a *12 ounce* Alnico[19] permanent magnet.

---

[18] A "klystron" is a special tube that generates microwave energy.
[19] "Alnico" is a high performance, but commonly used permanent magnet material.

The whole assembly, including the double Dewar, wave-guide coupling, maser cavity and associated microwave accessories weighed 25 pounds. A reduction in weight of 200 to 1!

The operation was completely stable and the figure of merit was improved by a factor of 10 over the conventional design. The maser's sensitivity to weak signals was also excellent.

I delivered the compact ruby maser to the United States Army Signal Corps on time and they installed it at the front end of a radar receiver. They were delighted at the performance and more practical design, which turned out to be far more impressive than they had hoped for.

## Cryogenics, the "Killer"

As much as this new maser design was considerably more practical than the prior 5,000-pound monster, state-of-the-art unit, it still needed liquid helium to operate properly. As described above, cryogenics, the technology that is required to cool a product to very low temperatures is, complex and costly. In fact, it's a real pain.

I was motivated to refine the maser a bit further, move the operating temperature upward, and make it still smaller. I developed a maser able to work with *only* liquid nitrogen cooling and thus only a single Dewar was needed. The unit weighed just four pounds.

I did my best to optimize the performance of the small unit, but, its weak signal detectability and gain-bandwidth product were not nearly as good as the liquid-helium-cooled maser, although comparable to the prior monster. This "miniature" unit still required cryogenics, albeit only liquid nitrogen. As a practical product, the solid-state maser was simply not very viable. It was vulnerable to any reasonable competition.

An electronic device called a parametric amplifier came on the scene with very good low signal sensitivity. Its performance was not quite up to a liquid-helium-cooled maser but it was considerably less complex and costly and, it could be operated at normal room temperature.

The ruby maser all but died. It became, in effect, a white elephant with current use limited to reception of weak signals from outer space.

Low-temperature physics has been and continues to be an extremely valuable tool for basic research. But the downside is that cryogenics is a "killer" when it comes to practical devices, especially when liquid helium is required.

For research, yes, but in no later *device* development was I willing to seriously consider a design that depended on cryogenics.

CHAPTER 6

# Building Blocks

Before continuing the story, I take a diversion into the basic physical principles underlying the operation of lasers to help the reader follow its chronology and development later in the text. This background will also clarify the tenuous connection between masers and lasers.

## Radiation and Atoms

According to the quantum theory of matter, atoms and molecules can only take on energy in discrete amounts. These species are described as occupying particular energy levels or quantum states.

As a helpful analogy, consider a room with a smooth top table and some marbles. The marbles are most stable when they are on the floor (on the ground). Similarly, when atoms are in their lowest stable state they are said to be in their *ground state*.

Now consider lifting one of the marbles off the floor and placing it on the table. It took some energy to lift the marble to the table height. That energy is stored in the marble as long as the marble remains on the table. But, we know that the marble is not stable on the tabletop. It is likely that the marble will roll off the table due to some vibration in the floor or, perhaps, from a tiny breeze of wind blowing through the window.

As the marble falls toward the floor and accelerates, it picks up kinetic (moving) energy equal to the stored energy that it had when it was on the table.

Atoms behave in a somewhat analogous way. An atom which has had energy imparted to it above its ground state is said to be in an *excited state*. By a process known as *spontaneous radiation*, this atom can arbitrarily return to the ground state and release its stored energy in the form of an emitted photon which, in turn, goes off in a random direction[20]. The electromagnetic waves associated with each randomly emitted photon have arbitrary phase relationships with respect to, the waves emitted by other spontaneously emitted photons.

*Spontaneous emission of radiation is, therefore, incoherent.*

In his famous 1916 treatise on radiation, Einstein came up with a new concept. He showed that atoms already in an excited state (marbles on the table) could lose their energy by another process, other than and in addition to, spontaneous emission of radiation.

He postulated that a photon that has the same energy that the atom has stored in its excited level could interact with this atom and induce, or *stimulate*, it to radiate its stored energy in the form of another photon. He called this new process *stimulated emission*.

The outgoing stimulated photon will have the same energy and travel in the same direction as, that of the stimulating photon.[21] The quantum theory analysis of the process shows that not only is the frequency of the electromagnetic radiation associated with the outgoing photon at the same frequency of the stimulating photon, but also the radiation waves are in step with each other.

*Stimulated emission of radiation is, therefore, coherent.*

How do atoms get into an excited state?

---

[20] Light (electromagnetic radiation) has, in a sense, a dual nature. Although it is a wave phenomenon, sometimes it is more convenient to consider light as a beam of particles called photons. Both representations can be shown to be mathematically equivalent.

[21] Using the previous analogy, a marble on the table struck squarely by another marble goes off, initially, in the same direction as that of the striking marble.

There are a number of ways that this can happen, but for our purposes here let us consider a special case. The case in question is one in which a photon of just the right energy[22] interacts with an atom in its ground state. The photon energy could be absorbed by the atom and thereby, raise it (the atom) into an excited state. This process just described is referred to as induced, or *stimulated absorption.*

To recapitulate: If an atom is in its ground state and a photon (from a light beam) happens to have just the right energy corresponding to one of the atom's allowed energy levels, that photon may induce the atom to absorb the photon's energy and thus raise it to an excited level by stimulated absorption.

If the excited atom is left on its own, it will radiate a photon randomly and be returned to the ground state. This *randomly* emitted photon is spontaneous, *incoherent,* radiation.

*But*, if a photon interacts with the *excited* atom, again of just the right energy, *before* the atom has a chance to emit its spontaneous emission, then alternatively, the atom can lose its energy by emitting a photon in the same direction and phase as the stimulating photon.

## The "Inverted Population" and "Negative Temperature"

You can see from the discussion above that photons can induce atoms in their ground state to absorb the photon's energy. Yet, these same photons can induce atoms in an excited state to give up their energy.

So, a photon interacting with an atom can cause *both* stimulated *absorption* and stimulated *emission.* Which dominates?

According to principles elucidated in Einstein's radiation theory, the probability of *absorption* is the same as the probability of *emission.* As a result, the absorption process normally dominates since most of the atoms lie in their stable ground state. That is, a stream of photons will be absorbed by the high density of atoms in their ground state and can only induce the very few atoms that happen to be in excited states to radiate. This is the normal status quo (more marbles on the floor than on the table top). In this case, Einstein's stimulated emission is of little or no consequence.

----

[22] "The right energy" is the condition where the photon energy is exactly equal to the energy needed to raise the atom from its ground state up to one of its excited states (the energy needed to raise the marble from the floor to the table top)

But ... What if we could figure out a way to change the status quo? What if we arrange to somehow get an assemblage of atoms (in a solid, liquid, or gas) to have *more* atoms in their *excited* states than in their lower or ground states?[23]

Now, when a stream of photons with the right energy interacts with the material, there is *more* stimulated *emission* than there is stimulated absorption. Such a system will actually *amplify* instead of absorb electromagnetic radiation of the right frequency.[24]

The density of atoms in a particular energy state is often referred to as its *population*. The unusual, unnatural condition whereby there are more atoms in an excited state than there are in some lower state (not necessarily the ground state), is called an *inverted population*, a condition backwards from what we find in nature.[25]

The inverted population is the fundamental basis of laser operation. Since a material in such a condition is an amplifying medium, we can see how the acronym *laser* is constructed: *light **a**mplification by **s**timulated **e**mission of **r**adiation*.

How do we achieve an inverted population? This is a crucial question. Since a material with an inverted population can amplify, that is, produce more energy than there was before, it is necessary to supply an external source of excitation. Alas, in science too, "there is no free lunch."

The detail of just how to solve that problem, to accomplish the none-too-easy task of achieving an inverted population, is key to the successful realization of a laser.

### The Laser Condition

Whereas getting an inverted population is the absolutely necessary basic requirement for possible laser operation, it is by no means sufficient in and of itself. Not only must the unnatural condition of an inverted population be devised, but also the *magnitude* of that population inversion must be large enough to overcome inherent practical limitations.

---

[23] More marbles on the table top than on the floor.
[24] The frequency of an electromagnetic wave and the energy of its associated photons are connected by a fundamental parameter known as *Planck's constant*—the higher the wave frequency, the higher the photon energy.
[25] Equations used in the analysis of population densities include the effective temperature of the system. Physicists often use the term *negative temperature* to account for and describe a system with an inverted population.

The *amount* of net stimulated emission must exceed the amount of spontaneous emission. Lastly, *but most important*, to achieve coherent light the *magnitude* of the amplification in the potential laser medium must be of sufficient proportions to overcome the inevitable losses in any practical associated structure (called a resonator).

In the case of some laser types, notably most gas lasers, this latter condition can be as or even more formidable a task to accomplish as the one to produce an inverted population.

CHAPTER 7

# Laser Chronology

## Stimulated Emission Proposals

Several proposals emerged over time attempting to devise ways to achieve amplification or oscillation by means of *stimulated emission of radiation*. The Russian physicist V. A. Fabricant made the earliest and highly notable laser proposal.

In 1940, writing in his doctoral dissertation, Fabricant specified the conditions needed for amplification of light via stimulated emission. He appreciated the concept of an inverted population and the concept of coupling such inverted population medium to a resonant structure (resonator). He proposed using a gaseous electrical discharge to achieve laser action as one possibility. Later, he proposed the use of a helium discharge lamp to optically pump the gaseous form of the basic chemical element cesium.

Although Fabricant was not successful in achieving coherent light, his analytical and experimental work preceded the demonstration of, any other stimulated emission device.

Scientists Purcell and Pound were the first to report evidence of net stimulated emission in 1951. Their observation, laying in the radio spectrum, far away from light frequencies, was a by product of their pioneering developments in the techniques of nuclear induction, the foundation for Magnetic Resonant Imaging.

In 1953, Joseph Weber, at the University of Maryland, published a proposal for a microwave amplifier that was based on stimulated emission in a paramagnetic solid.

## The Maser, an Interlude on the Way to Laser

The first achievement of a working device that utilized stimulated emission as its operating principle was a microwave oscillator/amplifier. That device used a beam of ammonia molecules as the working medium. The design details were worked out simultaneously by the collaborating scientists Nikolai Basov and Alexander Prokhorov at the Lebedev Institute in the Soviet Union. They were in parallel with but independent of the team of C.H. Townes and associates at Columbia University in the United States.[26]

In 1954, the Townes group reduced their design to practice and dubbed the device a *maser*, which is an acronym for *microwave amplification by stimulated emission of radiation*. In 1964, Basov, Prokhorov and Townes shared a Nobel Prize, for their ammonia maser work.

The ammonia beam maser emitted radiation at a power level of one ten-billionth of one watt! At the time the ammonia maser was developed, there were already many other ways to generate far larger amounts of coherent microwave power, from milliwatts to megawatts.[27] These other means were infinitely simpler, more efficient and certainly less costly. Examples of such microwave generators included exotic vacuum tube devices known as klystrons, traveling wave tubes and magnetrons. A one thousand-watt magnetron is the heat source in your microwave oven.

The ammonia beam maser was not a particularly useful or practical amplifier. Its operation was limited to the resonant frequency of the ammonia molecule and could only be used at barely detectable power levels. At first, it seemed to offer the possibility of a very accurate reference frequency and time standard. However, this maser wasn't much more precise than a well-designed electronic *quartz-crystal oscillator*, which is infinitely simpler and cheaper to realize.

More important, other atomic time standards soon came along with accuracy levels some ten thousand times greater than the ammonia beam maser. Consequently, interest in the ammonia maser died out after a short life span.

---

[26] J.P. Gordon, H.J. Zeiger and C.H. Townes.
[27] A milliwatt is one one-thousandth of one watt; a megawatt is one million watts.

A totally different kind of maser that used certain solid-state crystals subjected to a large magnetic field was developed subsequent to the ammonia-beam maser. This solid-state maser had the advantage— unlike the ammonia beam maser—that it could be tuned and designed to operate over a range of microwave frequencies. It had unusually high sensitivity to weak signals.

The concept and a specific design for a solid-state maser was detailed by Professor Nicolas Bloembergen at Harvard University. Then, along the lines suggested by Bloembergen, G. Feher and associates at Bell Telephone Labs built the first solid-state maser.[28] That maser used a very fragile crystalline material (gadolinium ethyl sulfate) as described by Bloembergen.

Soon afterward, Professor C. Kikuchi and coworkers at the University of Michigan developed and built, a solid-state maser using the very robust, man-made ruby crystal.

It was this Kikuchi ruby maser that I took over and developed from the 5000-pound monster to the more manageable 25-pound unit described in detail in the last chapter.

*The maser did not in any way extend the coherent electromagnetic spectrum. Also its use as an amplifier turned out to be impractical because cryogenic temperatures were required for proper operation.*

In the end, although the maser provided a very interesting bit of physics exploration for several years, it was no more than an interlude, if not a distraction, on the way to the laser. It was plainly a backward move from the work of Fabricant.

---

[28] H.E.D. Scovil, G. Feher and H. Seidel.

## Potassium Vapor Laser?

In August 1958, Arthur L. Schawlow at the Bell Telephone Laboratory, together with his brother-in-law Professor Charles H. Townes at Columbia University wrote a technical paper titled *Infrared And Optical Masers.*[29] Their paper was published in the December 1958 issue of the prestigious physics journal *Physical Review.* The cornerstone of this publication was a *proposal* for an infrared laser using as its working medium, the hot vapor[30] of the basic chemical element potassium. Even though the Schawlow-Townes potassium-vapor proposal proved to be unworkable, their paper has been much referenced and I believe, generally misunderstood.[31]

---

[29] The origin, use and, demise of the curious term, *optical maser* is explained in Chapter 19.

[30] The word vapor is another name for gas. Materials that are liquids or solids at normal room temperatures evaporate and the gaseous form is called vapor. For example, the gaseous water content in the air is water vapor. Steam that is created when water is boiled is also water vapor. The gas that is in equilibrium balance with potassium metal when it is heated is potassium vapor.

[31] This paper is critiqued and discussed in detail in Chapter 19.

CHAPTER 8

# Race to the Light

## Atmospheric Conditions

By the end of July, in the summer of 1959, I completed my work on the miniature, liquid-nitrogen ruby maser. Starting in early August, I reassembled my early incubative thoughts that had been interrupted and diverted, when I was enlisted into the ruby maser project. I began to devote full effort to consideration and analysis of my concepts for a laser.

There was already much activity underway at other laboratories. By now, the widely publicized 1958 Schawlow-Townes *Physical Review* publication had become a catalyst. Its effect was to release monies from government contract agencies as well as industrial and university research laboratories. Many scientists, not really scrutinizing the paper, were under the impression that the search for a laser was nothing more than simple implementation of ideas discussed in the Schawlow-Townes publication. This was a rather naïve and mistaken impression.

Laser activity was hot and heavy at the Columbia Radiation Laboratory where Charles Townes headed a group of five scientists (a government contract supported project), in pursuit of his co-authored potassium-vapor concept.

Bell Telephone Laboratories also had in process several well funded laser projects. One of these efforts was the work being done by a group of six scientists in Bell's solid-state physics section. That activity, spearheaded by Art Schawlow, reported to Albert M. Clogston.

Additionally, Bell Labs fostered two gas laser development groups; one headed by J.H. Sanders, on leave from Oxford University and another one headed by Ali Javan, a former Charles Townes student.

Work at other United States laboratories included a million-dollar US government funded program at TRG and, serious laser efforts at Massachusetts Institute of Technology (MIT), IBM, GE, RCA and Westinghouse. The laser hunt was on in European and Asian laboratories as well, including the important work in the Soviet Union at the Lebedev Institute headed by research scientists Basov and Prokhorov.

The TRG effort is worthy of special note. TRG was a small technology company founded by a group of scientists interested in the ideas of physicist Gordon Gould. Gould had been a graduate student at Columbia University at the same time that Schawlow and Townes wrote their proposal for a potassium-vapor laser.

By coincidence, Gould submitted a patent application for a vapor-laser system very similar to the plan outlined in the Schawlow-Townes proposal. The key difference in proposals was that Gould planned to use the vapor of the similar chemical element, sodium, for a working medium instead of potassium vapor as promoted by Schawlow-Townes. Gould and Schawlow-Townes were later to fight over who got the alkali vapor concept from whom. But, it didn't matter, neither system ever worked. More detail on the Gould patent is presented in Chapter 23.

During the cold war years, the United States was especially competitive with the Soviet Union. When the Russians successfully launched their Sputnik satellite in 1959, the U.S. Congress set up a new department, the Advanced Research Project Agency (ARPA). The congressional concept was to be aggressive in keeping the U.S. current with advanced research and hopefully, avoid such embarrassments in the future.

TRG submitted a contract proposal, based on Gould's concepts, to ARPA asking for $300,000. Since ARPA had a large new pot of money and was looking for places to "invest," they responded by awarding TRG a *one million dollar contract*![32]

---

[32] One million, 1959 U.S. dollars, is about five million year 2000 U.S. dollars.

The specific development efforts mentioned above were the high profile ones of which I was most aware. The point I'm making is that there was rather formidable global competition already in play. These efforts were well funded and very competently manned.

## The late entry

Why would I be willing to enter such a race?

The answer lies in my knowledge of the proposals that had been floated about. Obviously, I didn't know all the details of the work going on in the globally diverse laboratories. But, generally, the scientists who pursued these notions were not particularly secretive about what they were working on. They published and gave talks at conferences.

Notwithstanding the Schawlow-Townes publication and its attendant publicity, I found that the authors and conference presenters were only offering vague proposals. To be sure, this served as an exchange of information and stimulated ideas. Plainly, another purpose of these papers was to stake out claims. In any case, it didn't appear to me that any one was close to the answer. *The reality? No viable laser concept was yet in existence.*

As I look back, I was a little brash. I would be thrusting myself in a sense, into a technological Olympics. The competition was of the best quality and of international scope. But my competitive spirit won out. The challenge of working in the top league of such an exciting project, that had so many questions and problems to resolve, was very compelling to me.

*Keep in mind, it was not a given that anyone would ever succeed in making coherent light. It had never been done before!*

At least the Wright brothers could look up into the sky and see birds flying.

## Hughes' Reluctance

There was a complication. The Hughes Research Laboratory where I was working was not favorably inclined to fund my development. Hughes, by and large, is funded by U.S. government contracts. From the time that I joined Hughes until the spring of 1959 I had, in fact, been working under government funded contracts.

At the time in question, I was between contracts and my funding was from the Hughes General Research Funds. Even these General Research

Funds really came from the government, since Hughes was allowed to have such an entry in the overhead costing of their contracts. Hughes was free however, to use the funds as they wished. Not surprisingly, there was a lot of competition for the General Research Funds in the Hughes Laboratory and accordingly, my work was heavily scrutinized.

The Hughes aircraft business was dominated by military electronics. Why should Hughes be interested in a laser even in the highly unlikely event that I were successful and beat out the fierce competition. What would Hughes do with a laser?

I tried to ignore the lack of moral support and negativity and proceeded to begin work on my plans. But, what direction would I take?

## Possible Directions and Approaches

I was not inclined to join in and proceed down the road proposed by Schawlow and Townes. There was already a sizable contingent working on that specific idea and I wasn't inspired to be part of the "me too" crowd.

There were other reasons I avoided the alkali-vapor idea. Their plan was to make use of the very corrosive chemical element potassium[33] further exacerbated by requiring the potassium to be heated to cooking oven temperature.[34] The anticipation of dealing with such potential corrosion and impurity problems was not very appealing to me.

The most important consideration that kept me away from following along the Schawlow-Townes path was that my own analysis of their approach revealed severely flawed reasoning. In my opinion, the described system had little, if any, chance of success.[35]

Surprisingly, in spite of the poor prognosis, the alkali-metal vapor system proposed by Schawlow-Townes (and Gould) was a popular directional approach pursued by a number of scientists.

The Bell Labs Scientists Ali Javan and J.H. Sanders, noted above, fostered another kind of proposal. Javan, Sanders (and Gordon Gould) independently of each other, envisioned the idea that excitation energy could be imparted to atoms in a gaseous state by

---

[33] The chemical alkali elements, of which potassium is a representative, are attributed with very high chemical reactivity, so much so, that they cannot be safely handled with bare hands. A piece of alkali metal dropped into water starts a fire.
[34] Chemical activity increases rapidly when the temperature rises.
[35] I back up my view of the Schawlow-Townes proposal in Chapter 19.

collisions with other atoms and electrons in an electrical discharge. Their proposed laser would function something like a neon sign. They hoped not only to arrive at an inverted population, but to also have enough gain to make laser operation possible.

It was natural for me to seriously consider working on a gaseous system. I could use techniques that I had learned while preparing my doctoral thesis at Stanford. These areas included vacuum systems, gas handling and, the excitation of atoms by collisions with electrons.

But, I also learned from my Stanford experiences that the processes in an electrical discharge are highly complex. The probability of an atom being excited to a particular energy level is difficult to calculate and determine. The number of energy levels that the atoms and ions can be excited into is very large. Many possibilities exist for these excited species to change their states and cascade into other levels with hard-to-determine branching ratios. The number of possibilities is enormous, and even with the modern computers of today, this problem would not be very amenable to a thorough *quantitative* analysis.

I use the word quantitative in the sense that the important aspects of a system can be described in detail with specific value numbers for the parameters that count. Only in this way do we have the information to arrive at a concrete design and evaluate its practical feasibility.

In contrast, a *qualitative* proposal leaves open much of the specifics. Many qualitative proposals are not workable when the specifics are found and proper calculations made. In any case, there is no way to evaluate a qualitative proposal for feasibility or practicability. In order to blossom, these ideas would need: exploration, measurements, quantitative calculation, sound analysis and design.

To elaborate on that thought, consider the following example. An aircraft proposal could state that all that is needed to make a flyable airplane are some wings, a fuselage, an engine and a propulsion system. Such a *qualitative* proposal does *not* tell how to make an airplane that will fly successfully.

It was only when the Wright brothers determined the specifics of the size and shape of the wings; the size, pitch, shape and the required rpm for the propeller; and, the weight and power of the required engine, that they were able to make a quantitative and correct analysis of whether their aircraft design was flyable or not.

The physics suggested by Javan and Sanders was interesting in principle, but they gave no specifics. Since much of the needed design data could not be calculated, they would have to perform many elaborate experiments to arrive at a possible workable design.

It was obvious that they would need to spend endless hours varying many parameters such as discharge current, gas pressure, pressure ratios of mixtures of gases, the size of the gas vessel and more ... *and they did*. They could not even predict with confidence at which wavelength the laser would operate, if indeed it did work at all.

I also, therefore, declined the gas laser approach.

## Strategy Guidelines; the Thought Process

Since I enjoy trying to find answers to tough problems, why was I so studiously avoiding the systems with difficult solutions? Was I not up to the tasks at hand? Didn't I have the wherewithal to take these particular challenges on? Was I frightened away too easily?

No, my reasoning was adamant on the need to focus. It is difficult for me to convey the specter of working on a problem that has never before been solved and, in spite of an optimistic outlook, there was the nagging doubt of whether there will ever be a solution. The practicality problems might ever prevent it from coming to fruition.

We know *now* that many kinds of lasers can be made. But back then, in 1959, we *didn't* know. We didn't even know with any confidence if it was really possible to make a laser at all. If it was that easy (although it seems that way now), the efforts of the two prior years by the well funded crack teams of Schawlow, Townes, Sanders, Javan, Gould and others would, surely have already have produced a laser.

My strategy was to limit myself to potential solutions to the making of a laser that did not have appreciable distractions in the design. That way I could focus strictly on just the laser problem itself. For example, in Chapter 19, you will see that only a grossly inadequate pumping lamp was readily available for the experiment on the envisioned potassium vapor laser. It would have taken a major lamp development program to overcome that deficiency.

I have discussed the major empirical (trial and error) program necessary to get a gaseous system into a condition of inverted population. Additionally, in a gaseous system, the *magnitude* of the inverted population could be a major problem. Indeed, the gain levels in the first gas laser were so miniscule that a special super-reflection mirror was needed to make it work.[36]

---

[36] A new immature technology called multilayer dielectric coating had to be employed to develop that special mirror.

## The Crystal Bias

As is apparent, I was reluctant to work on alkali-vapor or gas discharge systems; so what *was* I going to work on?

Consistent with my strategy guidelines of no design distractions, I chose to work with *solid-state crystals*. The main appeal that solids held for me was simplicity. By that, I mean simple in analysis and understanding and, simple in device conception.

In contrast to a gas discharge, the energy level diagram in an appropriate crystal is very limited. There are relatively few possibilities for the energy states, and by and large, the pertinent parameters for a potential laser candidate are amenable to a combination of calculations and relatively straightforward direct measurements. If an appropriate model were devised, it would be possible to *quantitatively* analyze the system.

Another advantage, in principle, to a solid crystal is its relatively high *gain coefficient*. By that, I mean the amplification in a given length of material is of reasonable proportions. This meant that the laser medium could be relatively small in size and short in extent and, I would not have the problem of developing or depending on the use of special mirrors. Indeed, my first laser used a crystal that was only 2 cm (three-quarters inch) long.

By contrast, the gain coefficient in the first *gas laser* was so low, even with the help of super-mirrors it could not function at a length of 60 cm (2 feet long). It was only after the length was increased to 100 cm (40 inches) that it could be made to work.

I was also intrigued with the concept of a solid medium since I would not have to deal with vacuum pumps, impurity problems and gas handling apparatus, or complex mirror mechanisms. I could put simple silver mirror coatings directly on the crystal as I had done with my small ruby maser. The bottom line was that, in principle, a solid crystal laser could be designed to be very simple, compact and rugged.

Some potential crystal lasers would require cooling the crystal to very low temperatures. As I have emphatically expressed earlier, *I was adamant about avoiding a device solution that required cryogenics.* I didn't care to work on another white elephant like the ruby maser.

It is curious that some authors of laser history say I was obsessed with making a *practical* laser, in contrast to other laser researchers who were content to emphasize just the physics in their attempt to demonstrate coherent light. One would think it would be to my credit if I could achieve both coherent light *and* practicality.

But, that isn't the point. *I was not obsessed with practicality, I was obsessed with simplicity.* It is a truism though; things that are simple are also apt to be more practical. (Consider the small simple sealed-off tube in my thesis experiment and the compact 25-pound ruby maser.)

### Profile of a Pink Ruby

My first choice to study and contemplate was that of a *ruby crystal.*

What, exactly, is ruby?

Ruby is the result when a water-clear crystal of aluminum oxide is *doped*[37] with a small amount of chromium oxide impurity. It is the chromium that is responsible for the red color. The impurity free, transparent aluminum oxide crystal is very useful in industry, it is referred to as clear sapphire.

In the case of the ruby gemstone, the chromium impurity level is about 0.5% (one part in 200). Even this low level of chromium oxide is able to impart the deep red color to the crystal. Interestingly, the sapphire and ruby gemstones are chemically almost identical to each other. They are examples of the same mineral called corundum. The only difference between them is that the gem sapphire has small amounts of iron and titanium impurities in the aluminum oxide crystals. It is these iron and titanium impurities that are responsible for the classic blue coloration of the sapphire gem.

Rubies and sapphires are extremely rugged crystals and among the hardest of gems. Diamond is the only gem that is harder and therefore able to scratch ruby or sapphire.

The rubies used for devices are usually not natural gemstones but are man-made. Under controlled laboratory conditions, much more optically perfect crystals can be "grown"[38] which are also almost totally free of extraneous unwanted impurities compared to ruby gemstones.

The chromium concentration in device rubies is adjusted in the growth process to be around ten times less than in the gemstones (about one part in 2000). Because of the low chromium level in these crystals they display a lighter red color than gemstone ruby and are referred to as *pink ruby.*

---

[37] The word *doped* in the context of crystal growth refers to the addition of controlled amounts of impurities.
[38] The ruby crystal growth process is explained in Chapter 20.

## Ruby's Potential

Why choose ruby as a potential laser candidate?

To begin, I already had some rubies in my laboratory, which were left over from my work on the ruby maser. But, more important, I was also quite familiar with and fascinated by the interesting optical properties of the crystal.[39] Ruby is a fluorescent mineral; if an ultraviolet light is shined on a ruby, it will glow with deep red fluorescence. I learned about the energy level structure in crystalline ruby from a paper written by two Japanese spectroscopists. [40]

One day while doing preliminary work with some fluorescent crystals (not just ruby), I used a short-wave ultraviolet source and observed the fluorescence directly with my eyes. George Birnbaum, my immediate supervisor had just walked into the lab. I showed him a glowing ruby and I facetiously said:

"Hey George, look, here is a laser." He replied "yeah, yeah, sure!"

I only had the gleam of my idea at that time that eventually I really would be able to make a ruby *lase*.

That same night, I woke up at about two in the morning with intense pain and a feeling of sand in my eyes. My wife and I went to the hospital emergency room, where I was diagnosed with burnt eyeballs. I hadn't protected myself from the ultraviolet radiation from the lamp. Fortunately, my eyes were back to normal in a few days.

Ruby not only absorbs and fluoresces under ultraviolet light, but it also gives off a red glow when either blue or green light is shined upon it. It is from these blue and green absorption bands that ruby receives its red color. A ruby crystal absorbs the blue and green parts of the broad white daylight spectrum leaving the red light, which is not absorbed, to shine through.

What is happening here?

When a green photon impinges on and is absorbed by the ruby, a chromium impurity ion is raised from its ground state into a broad, excited band. Although the chromium ion has the possibility of radiating by spontaneous emission from that excited level, another process comes into play. The competing process uses the thermal vibrations of the crystal lattice to interact with the excited ion and

---

[39] It is, perhaps, somewhat confusing that ruby can be used for masers as well as lasers. That is a coincidence; there is no direct connection between the two.
[40] Saturo Sagano and Y. Tanabe.

deposit most of the excitation energy to another slightly lower excited level of the ruby chromium ion where it stays for a while. This latter process is much more probable and dominates.

The energy from this third level[41] is radiated as spontaneous incoherent emission. This spontaneous emission is made up of red photons and is the observed fluorescence. The level where the fluorescence emanates is sometimes called a *metastable level,* since the chromium ions linger in that energy state for a comparatively long time before they radiate red photons.[42]

The emitted red photons have less energy than the green photons that started the process. The missing lost energy is deposited in the ruby crystal in the form of heat. Under high levels of excitation the ruby gets hot.

When I first started to examine the optical properties of ruby in some detail, I did not necessarily favor its serious use for a laser. I had been thinking, for quite some time, that within the class of materials known as fluorescent solids there could be some good potential candidates for a laser. I continued to study the ruby at first, merely because it was a representative of that class of materials.

**Laser Genotype**

I developed a model that could be mathematically analyzed and I set up what are called *kinetic equations* to take into account the various mechanisms taking place in the fluorescent process. I also set up simple intuitive criteria for establishing the condition for laser action.

*This model and these equations have subsequently become a standard way for others to analyze crystal lasers.*

I was able to determine which material parameters were important and relevant to a laser by getting the solution to the equations describing the model. Although some of these material properties were available in the published literature, other properties would have to be directly measured or calculated from other measurements.

Using the known and estimated values for the pertinent parameters in ruby, I made some preliminary calculations. I found that ruby would require a very bright pump lamp to excite the crystal sufficiently to allow laser action to take place.

---

[41] The second level is the broad green band
[42] In Chapter 9, I offer an extension of the marble on the table analogy to elucidate the fluorescent process.

The brightness of a lamp is an important parameter for lasers. It is a measure of not the total power radiated by the lamp, but rather the power per unit area. In other words, brightness is the *concentration* of the radiated power.

To illustrate the point, consider the following examples. A fluorescent light bulb is quite efficient but not very bright since the light is radiated from a fairly large area. On the other hand, a tungsten light bulb is not as efficient as the fluorescent bulb, but much brighter since the light radiates from a tiny filament. This filament is so *bright* that it is uncomfortable to look at it directly. Tungsten halogen lamps are brighter yet. The very brightest optical sources available are arc lamps. The brightest of these are carbon arcs (Hollywood Klieg lights) and mercury arc lamps.

Because of the very tough brightness requirement for the ruby, I decided to broaden my scope of potential candidates. I wanted to see if there were some other crystals that might have less demanding requirements and hence, might be more suitable laser candidates than ruby.

There was a fair amount of published data on the fluorescence spectra of crystals doped with a class of chemical elements known as the *rare earths*. They got that name because many members of that family are indeed quite rare. These elements are listed as a group in the chemical periodic table.

One of these rare earth elements is gadolinium. The gadolinium ion fluoresces in the ultraviolet part of the spectrum with some very sharp lines. I became particularly intrigued with the possible use of the gadolinium ion in a suitable crystal lattice as a potential material for a laser.

I was being a little greedy here. It would be an important development if I could make coherent light. But, with gadolinium, if it worked, I would get ultraviolet. Then, if I were successful, the jump in the coherent spectrum would be more like 25,000 times instead of *only* 10,000 times!

As I studied that concept further, my calculations showed that gadolinium doped crystals would be even harder to make *lase* than ruby. So, I went back to ruby to take a better look and ponder that problem.

With my parents, before Estelle was born.

With my sister Estelle

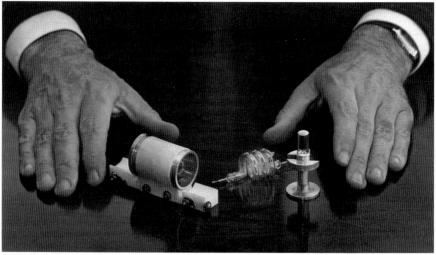

The real first laser.

ATOMIC RADIO-LIGHT -- Man has created a source of "coherent" light for the first time in history, a new electronic device called a laser (from Light Amplification by Stimulated Emission of Radiation), a Hughes Aircraft Company scientist has announced. Above, Dr. Theodore H. Maiman of Hughes Research Laboratories, where the scientific breakthrough was achieved, studies the laser's main parts, a light source surrounding a rod of synthetic ruby crystal through which excited atoms generate the intense beam. The laser projects the radio spectrum to 500,000 billion cycles, "lighting" the way for improved space communications and increasing the number of communications channels.

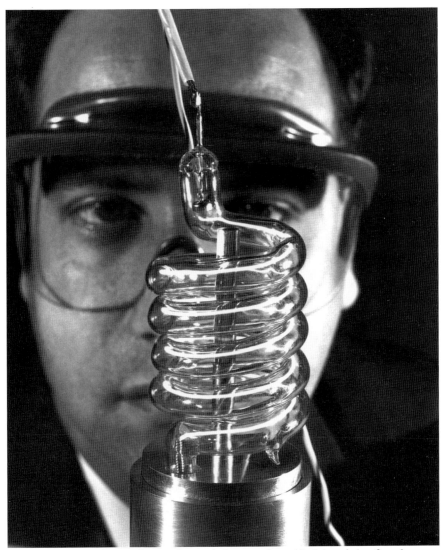

The July 1960 news release showed the much copied 'not' the first laser.

Attending a White House ceremony receiving the Fannie and John Hertz
Award from President Lyndon B. Johnson

A 1980 TRW news release photo at Lawrence Livermore Labs shows the
evolution of their 'Nova' from the first laser.

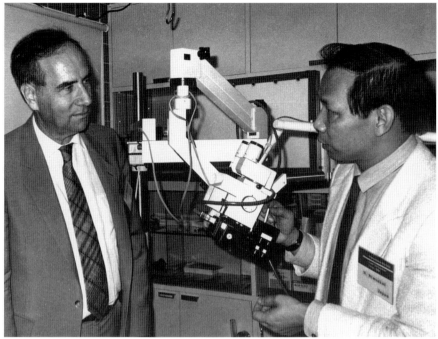

Laser plastic surgeon Nurong Nimsakul, M.D., at the International Institute of Laser Medicine, Japan

At the opening of the Cincinnati Laser Center at Deaconess. On the left is Hospital CEO E. Anthony Woods, with LCA Vision President Dr. Stephen Joffe.

A happy time with my daughter Sheri (1980)

Inducted into the
National Inventors
Hall of Fame, 1984

Matsushita presents me with the Japan Prize. Seated far right is Emperor
Akihito, then Crown Prince.

A warm greeting from Empress Michiko of Japan.
Emperor Akihito (far left) proudly looking on.

In Los Angeles celebrating the Japan Prize with close friends. From left to right: Bob and Terracea Hellwarth; Mike and Barbara Barnoski; Larry Cohen (hidden); Kathleen and myself; Lilianne and Lawrence McCain; Reba and Bernie Soffer.

With Mike and Barbara Barnoski on invited lecture in Japan. Mike nominated me for the Japan Prize.

CHAPTER 9

# Three Levels Can't Work

## Shawanga Lodge Conference

In the middle of September, that same year (1959), I went to a professional meeting. It was a conference organized by a committee headed by Charles Townes. It was sponsored and set up by the United States Office of Naval Research. This conference was held at the Shawanga Lodge, High View, New York, on September 14-16, 1959. The conference was titled Quantum Electronics—Resonance Phenomena.

Indicative of the level of interest in the pursuit of the first laser, 163 scientists working in the field of masers and or working toward laser ideas attended this conference. The US attendees included Bell Telephone Laboratories with the largest turnout—17 people, followed by MIT's Lincoln Labs with 7 (there were another 5 from MIT), followed by Columbia University, IBM and Westinghouse each with 5 people and GE, RCA and Hughes, with 4 each.

Supportive of the global nature of interest in the symposium subject matter, there were conference attendees from Canada, France, Russia, Britain, Switzerland, Germany, Holland, Japan, Sweden and Israel.

The Shawanga Lodge meeting took place more than a year after Schawlow and Townes had widely circulated their famous paper on *Optical and Infrared Masers.*

Observation: If the Schawlow-Townes 1958 *Physical Review* publication had truly set down the principles and teachings of lasers, one would have expected that by the time of the Shawanga Lodge Conference there would be at least one or two lasers reported on at that conference. On the contrary; *there were not any lasers reported on in the 67 papers presented at the Shawanga Lodge Meeting.*

The fact that, as yet, there was no viable laser concept was aptly indicated in the paper presented at the symposium by Art Schawlow himself. In his paper, Schawlow started out his presentation by saying:

*"As yet, nobody knows for sure what form a practical source of infrared or optical radiation will take."*

Obviously, the attainment of coherent light was turning out to be more difficult than originally envisioned by Schawlow and Townes in their *Physical Review* paper. They had not successfully instructed *anyone* on *how* to achieve a laser, including themselves.

*New concepts, much more computation, analysis and ingenuity were going to be needed before anyone would be able to create a laser.*

There were many suggestions and speculations at the conference on what form a laser might take, but, these were all couched in "possibly, maybe, could be, etc." Nothing specific, no definite direction, except that Schawlow again presented the hapless potassium-pumped-potassium vapor proposal.

Clearly, this continued to be the Schawlow-Townes preferred direction, even after one year's work on it to no avail. Based on the progress report on this system at the conference, the discrepancies between the potassium discharge lamp and the low-pressure potassium absorption cell had not yet been discovered.[43] The occurrence of impurity problems were reported, however.

## The Schawlow Goof

Schawlow made several conceptual errors in the presentation of his paper at the conference.

Quote from the conference proceedings, Schawlow wrote, *"For example, consider the optical spectrum of ruby, i.e. $Cr^{+3}$ in $Al_2O_3$. There is a broad absorption band in the green and others in the ultra violet. When excited through these bands, the crystal emits a moderate number of sharp lines in the deep red. The two strongest lines (at 6919A and 6934A) go to*

---

[43] In my analysis of the Schawlow-Townes proposal, in Chapter 19, I argue that this was a fatal flaw in their idea.

*the ground state, so that they will always have more atoms in their lower state and are not suitable, for Maser [Laser] action (emphasis added)."*

The wavelengths[44] quoted by Schawlow (6919A and 6934A) are the wavelengths of the fluorescence only when ruby is cryogenically cooled! I have to conclude that he was out of hand dismissing the possibility of room temperature operation (6934A and 6943A) for pink ruby.[45]

More important: always? It's probably a good rule in science to: *never say never, or, … always!*

I sat in on the actual paper presentation. In his oral remarks, Schawlow pressed his point and argued, "You know that you would *not* be able to deplete the ground state population because the crystal would be bleached." On that count, he was correct, the crystal *would* be bleached. But, that is not a convincing argument. I'm not aware of any law of physics that would be violated by this and he didn't offer any.

*I was utterly amazed to hear this line of reasoning.*

Schawlow didn't offer any specific calculation to back up his contention. He had obviously not gone through the development of an analytical model and was arguing without working out the details. But, as we know, the devil is in the details.

*Art Schawlow was incorrect!*

Schawlow insisted, as did most other early laser researchers, that three-level fluorescent solids were not viable candidates for laser operation. What was needed, they contended, was a so called, *four-level system.*

## The Meaning of Three-Level and Four-Level Lasers

In order to understand the concept of three-levels and four-levels, recall the analogy of the marbles and the table. This time consider that the table has a trough going around it just below the tabletop. The trough has a few holes just big enough to pass one marble at a time.

---

[44] Physicists who work in the optical part of the spectrum often speak of the wavelength of the electromagnetic radiation. What is wavelength? If you were to drop a pebble into a quiet pond you would expect to see a ripple of waves traveling away from the stone. The distance between adjacent crests of the waves corresponds to their wavelength. Waves that oscillate at a higher frequency have the wave crests closer together. Consequently, higher frequencies have shorter wavelengths. If we specify one of these terms (either frequency or wavelength), we automatically know the other one.

[45] The wavelength (frequency) of the ruby red fluorescence changes with temperature. When Art Schawlow specified the ruby wavelength in his discussion, I was able to discern that he had cryogenic temperatures in mind.

When a marble is lifted onto the tabletop (atom in an excited state), the marble cannot fall directly to the floor. Instead, it rolls into the trough and, after some delay, finally finds one of the holes in the trough and falls to the ground.

In the case of the ruby crystal, the tabletop corresponds to the green absorption band and the trough represents the *metastable* level. Marbles falling through the holes are the red fluorescent photons. Now remember the basic laser condition. We must create an *inverted population* between two levels. If we are aiming for a laser at the red wavelength, then *more* marbles must be stacked up in the trough then there are on the floor.

But before we add any excitation to the ruby (green photons raising the marbles up to the tabletop), all the marbles are on the floor. We have our work cut out for us. What saves the day or at least gives us a fighting chance, is that the trough has only a few holes for the marbles to fall through; the marbles get "hung up." If we put marbles on the table at a fast enough rate, the build up in the trough will indeed get more marbles in the trough than are left on the floor—an inverted population.

*Note, that in this three-level system, we need to move more than half of the marbles off the floor to get to an inverted population.* Suppose that we start out with 100 marbles on the floor and manage to move them at a fast enough rate to overcome the "leak" of marbles falling through the trough. If we can manage to put for example, 51 marbles in the trough, we would be left with 49 marbles on the floor. We have our sought after inverted population: there are two more marbles in the upper level (the trough) then there are on the floor (ground state). That was tough, but attainable.

We can carry the analogy further to account for a so-called four level system. Suppose we bring a low flat bench near the table. As before, without excitation, essentially all the marbles are on the floor. When the exciting light impinges on the system, again, marbles are lifted off the floor to the tabletop and roll off into the trough. What is different this time is that there is now a lower level—the bench level—that is essentially empty. Few marbles are needed in the trough in order to realize an inverted population *with respect to the bench level*. It is no longer necessary to take more than half the marbles out of the ground state (floor).

*In principle,* it appears that a four-level system is superior to a three-level system. You would surmise that it would require significantly less excitation (we call it pumping power) to get just a few marbles in the trough instead of a requirement to remove more than half the marbles off the floor. Again, the devil is in the details.

Where do we get the fourth level, that lower bench level? We need to find a material that has the fourth level available. But, the four-level material candidate may have other properties that are not particularly wanted. For example, the fourth level may lie too low and not really be empty.[46] To benefit from the fourth level it might be necessary to *cryogenically* cool the material. In that case, the fourth level advantage could be obliterated. As discussed in the maser chapter, it takes a tremendous amount of energy to make, store and handle cryogenic fluids. Cryogenics extracts a big price in complexity and cost.

The point is aptly demonstrated by the following. As noted above, Art Schawlow was convinced that pink ruby (0.05 % chromium concentration) was not a viable laser material. Instead, he offered dark ruby (0.5 % chromium).[47] He argued correctly, that dark ruby is a different material than pink ruby. It's ten times higher chromium concentration produces extra levels (satellite levels). Schawlow admits that broad emission lines with low quantum efficiency plague the dark ruby material. *But he is totally mesmerized by the fact that dark ruby is an example of the coveted four-level system.*

He was undeterred that the dark ruby would need to be cooled cryogenically with liquid helium to achieve four-level behavior. Again, without offering any quantitative calculations to back it up, he expected that the dark ruby, unlike the pink ruby, would require only modest, easily achievable excitation.

Seven months after I built the first laser, several researchers (including Schawlow) adopted the same configuration that was used in my original laser to make dark ruby lase. However, even with the advantage of cryogenic cooling, *the dark ruby required the same excitation level as the pink ruby.*

Again, Schawlow was incorrect, four levels didn't buy anything.

I had some mixed reactions to Schawlow's presentation. I certainly didn't believe the validity of his arguments since my own *quantitative* calculations led me to different conclusions. I knew that my concepts would be difficult to achieve, but by no means impossible.

*Why didn't I say anything?*

---

[46] Strictly speaking, a material at any finite temperature above absolute zero has some of its atoms in low-lying energy levels, in this case, the bench level. The degree to which this happens, in fact, does depend on the temperature.
[47] A detailed description of the composition of ruby, its connection to the gemstone and how, man-made ruby is "grown" follows in a later chapter.

Two reasons. First, I wasn't that sure of myself that I was willing to take on a scientist with the stature of an Art Schawlow. The other reason lay with my competitive spirit. Why tip off the opposition?

I have to admit, as I sat through the Schawlow lecture at this Shawanga Lodge Conference, that I was only in the preliminary stage of my thinking. I didn't appreciate that it would only be another eight months before I would be successful in bringing into the world the first laser using the condemned pink ruby material.

### Some Spin Control

In a documented interview[48], Schawlow declared, "But I guess I was the first to propose ruby. It may well be that I'd drawn Maiman's attention to ruby by *mentioning* in various places, that we might be able to use this dark ruby."[49]

Actually, Schawlow's misstatements at the Shawanga Lodge Meeting came back to haunt him. Members of the scientific community familiar with the facts circulated a joke: *"Schawlow is buying up all the copies of the Shawanga Lodge Conference Proceedings and burning them."*

### The Schawlow Ripple Effect

George Birnbaum, my supervisor also attended the Shawanga conference. Since George was very cool on my laser project anyway, he now wanted to kill the project funding and cancel it altogether. Schawlow, a scientist held in high regard, had in effect, said it couldn't work.

I had quite a heated discussion and made some very loud noises as I argued adamantly with George to keep my Hughes funding. I knew that, in the end, I might not be successful in making a laser. But, I was convinced that my ideas for devising a laser were as good as, if not better than, any of the other ideas that I had heard about.

Fortunately, I had a good "track record" at Hughes and that won the day, at least long enough to get me sufficient reprieve on the funding.

I might add that at some point during the development, Dick Daly, a vice president at TRG, visited the Hughes Research laboratory. He remarked rather facetiously in a conversation: "Well, why don't you

---

[48] Laser Pioneer Interviews, *High Tech Publications, Inc.* December 1985.
[49] In that same interview with *Laser Pioneers*, Schawlow admitted that he had unsuccessfully tried to make a dark ruby lase using a 25 joule (watt-second) flashlamp. Again, Art failed to make valid calculations. *He was short in pumping power by a factor of some 100 times!*

work on ruby?" Ha-Ha! Apparently, TRG had also considered ruby and, along with Art Schawlow, had unwisely abandoned it.

Although I was not the only one to consider the ruby's candidacy for laser action, I was the only one that analyzed ruby in enough *detail* to have the confidence to stick with it.

CHAPTER 10

# Obstacles and Solutions

### Irwin Wieder Distraction

As it happened, I did abandon ruby ... for a while. But it was not because of Schawlow, not because of Daly, and not because of the pressure from George Birnbaum. It was because of Wieder.

Remember Irwin Wieder? He was the graduate student who I trained on my thesis apparatus so Willis Lamb could release me and sign off on my Ph.D.

Irv went to work at the Westinghouse Research Laboratory in Pittsburgh after he got his doctorate from Stanford. He too was doing some very interesting work with ruby, but not for a laser. He wanted to optically excite the ruby to make a better maser.[50] Wieder made a measurement of the quantum efficiency of the ruby fluorescence[51] and reported his results in the November 1959 issue of *Review of Scientific Instruments.*[52]

---

[50] Irwin Wieder did not succeed in making an optically pumped maser. But, in 1962, Don Devor, Irnee D'Haenens and Charlie Asawa did make such a device by optically exciting a ruby maser crystal with a ruby laser at Hughes.

[51] The quantum efficiency for a fluorescent crystal is the number of fluorescent photons emitted, divided by the number of pumping photons. That is, for every marble put on the table, how many marbles get into the trough and through the holes back to the ground. In the case of ruby, it would be the number of red photons radiated out, compared to the number of green photons absorbed.

[52] *The Review of Scientific Instruments,* Vol. 30, number 11, 995-996, November 1959.

Based on the results of his measurements, *Irv Wieder reported that the fluorescent quantum efficiency of ruby was only one percent.*

That number was very disturbing. I knew from the calculations based on my model that ruby would require a bright pumping source and consequently, that it would be quite difficult to induce laser action in the material. But, I determined that task was not impossible, as Schawlow had insisted.

However, my assumption was that ruby had a near 100% internal efficiency. *When I put Wieder's data into the calculations, ruby did, indeed, look next to impossible.*

I didn't question Irv's measurement: he had been my protégé at Stanford, so I trusted his results. I was discouraged and began to look elsewhere for other possibilities. But, as I looked around so to speak, I didn't find any obvious desirable system to pursue.

I decided to go back and take a closer look at ruby. I knew that I couldn't change the material's internal efficiency, that's fundamental to the crystal. But, on the other hand, I wanted to know what the problem was, where was the bottleneck?

## The Monochromator Hassle

About this time, I decided to order an instrument that could aid me in my measurements. This piece of equipment, called a mono-chromator, used a diffraction grating to filter light into one color at a time. The diffraction grating is a kind of optical filter. It does the same thing as a prism; it separates out the colors of the spectrum. However, the diffraction grating does a more precise job than a prism.

Bausch and Lomb made the particular monochromator that I was interested in. This was the exact monochromator that I had used in my thesis experiment at Stanford. It cost $1,500.

A signature from Harold Lyons, head of my Atomic Physics Department was required for this capital equipment acquisition. Harold didn't want to approve the monochromator purchase. Interestingly, at Stanford it hadn't been a problem.

Harold, as did George Birnbaum previously, also argued that I was beating a dead horse. Didn't Schawlow say that ruby couldn't work? You can't depopulate the ground state. Harold commented, "Why don't you work on something useful, like computers?" Once more, I was forced to defend the sensibility of my project. Fortunately, I was again successful in my arguments. I got my monochromator and was allowed to proceed with my experiments.

## The Ruby Obsession

Why did I keep hanging onto the ruby?

Ruby has many desirable qualities: It is a very stable, very rugged crystal to work with. It has some broad pumping bands that make it helpful to get a reasonable energy transfer from an incoherent pumping lamp and compared to some other crystals I considered, a working ruby laser would produce visible light.

The other crystal candidates (including the so called dark-ruby), besides less desirable operation in the infrared, required cryogenic cooling. If pink ruby did work, it could do so at room temperature.

What did I hope to accomplish by studying ruby further? Why didn't I just let go, abandon ruby and go on from there?

I couldn't *redesign* the ruby itself. My reasoning was that if I could understand *where* the ruby lost the 99 percent of its excitation, I might be guided in my search for other materials that retained the desirable features of ruby, but lacked what was looming as a fatal problem for this crystal.

## Redo the Fluorescence Measurement

I looked very critically at the fluorescence process of pink ruby in detail. As a result, I was able to devise experiments to measure the magnitude of perceived possible problems.

I followed through with the experiments, but, one after one, the possible leakage mechanisms that I checked for, didn't materialize. Puzzled, I decided to do an experiment to check the overall fluorescent efficiency myself.

*According to my measurements, I found ruby to have a fluorescent efficiency more like 75 percent as opposed to Wieder's reported one percent ... Fantastic!*

This new corrected data was an absolutely stunning turn of events. I was exhilarated and I started to get more confident and optimistic.

Ruby was back in the ball game! ... Or was it?

## The AH6 Design

I now had enough information that I could proceed to work out an actual laser design.

But how would I pump the ruby? What would be the ruby's shape and size?

I knew that I needed a very bright lamp. Among the brightest around, was a high-pressure mercury arc lamp, a General Electric AH6. In addition to being one of the brightest available laboratory lamps, it had the advantage of radiating most of its energy in the green and blue-violet part of the spectrum. This was a good match to what I needed for the ruby.

I drew up a paper design with the AH6 at the focus of an elliptic cylinder. A small ruby rod was to be mounted on the other focus of the elliptic cylinder.

What is an elliptic cylinder? Think of a hollow circular pipe. If we flatten that pipe a bit, then a cross section assumes a more oval shape (not exactly, but essentially an ellipse). Instead of the one center of curvature when it was a circle, the cross section now has two centers of curvature separated from each other. These two centers are called the foci of the ellipse.

It is a property of an elliptically shaped reflector that a point of light placed at one focus of the ellipse will be imaged at the other focus. The elliptic cylinder that I had in mind would be highly polished on its inner surface to a mirror finish.

But I had a problem. My paper analysis of the design showed that although it should work, it would only do so by a slim margin. I studied the design in more detail, looking for ways to optimize and improve it, but I couldn't convince myself that it was anything but marginal.

Why not build it anyway? After all, if it didn't work, as they say, "Back to the drawing board!"

It was my mental state. Even though I was reasonably confident of my calculations, the outside pressures were getting to me. Could everybody else be wrong when they said ruby was not a practical laser material?

I was also still hung up with "Could coherent light really be made? It has never been done before." What new phenomenon might I run into?

What if the potential laser wasn't working, but I was very close. How would I know if my design was not quite there or if I was encountering something more fundamental?

Although a minor consideration, it is a fact that the AH6 is a nasty lamp to work with. It's a 1,000-watt bulb that needs water cooling or very high-pressure air to operate and keep it from burning up (the air-cooled version is a BH6). Even with proper cooling, the lamp only has a life expectancy of 25 hours.

It didn't help that George Birnbaum was convinced that I was beating a dead horse.

I got a bit discouraged again. For me, it was hard to get very excited about a marginal design.

I stewed over the problem at hand. I started to think about other ways to look at the problem. I was frustrated, I felt that, on the one hand I was very close to an answer, but at the same time it was eluding me.

### Brightness Temperature

I went back to my analytical model. I pondered my options and decided to put the pumping lamp requirement for the ruby in a different form. I calculated the equivalent *black-body* temperature of a suitable pumping lamp.[53]

As an example, an ordinary tungsten light bulb is nearly an ideal black body with a brightness temperature of about 2,800 degrees Kelvin (2525 Celsius). Laboratory lights are often characterized this way, by an equivalent black body temperature.

The number that I calculated to have enough brightness capable of driving a ruby into laser action was close to 5,000 degrees Kelvin. That is a temperature similar to the surface of the sun!

In principle, I could make a solar collector (mirror or lens) and use it to focus sunlight onto the ruby, but again, it would be marginal.

Yet, once I put the pumping requirement in terms of brightness temperature, I began to think in a different way. I remembered reading an article about photographic strobe lamps, a camera's flash mechanism. The article said that strobe lamps could reach brightness temperatures of 8,000 degrees Kelvin or more!

*I now had my aha!*

---

[53] By that is meant the temperature to which a fictitious hot body would have to be heated to put out enough light to pump the ruby.

## The Pulsed Concept

Most scientists had been thinking in terms of a continuous laser. That was certainly my thinking to start with. But, why should I place such restrictions on myself?

At this juncture, I was only trying to demonstrate that coherent light could be made at all. Besides, a pulsed source is not only acceptable in many applications, it may even be preferable; for example: radar; welding; hole-drilling; scientific research and instrumentation; and high-speed photography, for which the strobe lamp was designed originally.

I went back to my analytical model, modified the equations to account for a pulsed light source, and then analyzed the results to guide me in the actual laser design. I had already determined that the most important parameter of the light source would be its brightness, that is, a lamp that maximized the power per unit area into the useful pump bands of the ruby.[54]

My calculations also instructed me that this lamp brightness requirement is largely independent of the ruby crystal dimensions and its chromium concentration over a reasonably wide range. The model assumption was that of a three-level system (appropriate to ruby) where the lower laser-energy level is the ground state.[55]

Next, I scoured every flashlamp catalog that I could find. One of the parameters usually given in these catalogues is the lumen output of the lamp. For my purposes this was a very pertinent parameter. The lumen is based on the spectral or color response of the human eye. By coincidence the main green pumping band for ruby is very similar to the human eye response.

I calculated the luminous intensity for promising candidates and found that the highest intensity (lumens divided by the radiating area of the lamp) came form three General Electric spiral shaped flashlamps, the FT-506, the FT-503/524, and the FT-623. The largest of these lamps, the FT-623 had the highest intensity of all the lamps that I found. The FT-503 was smaller and had, somewhat less intensity, while the FT-506 had still less intensity.

---

[54] For ruby, the useful pump radiation is primarily in the green and secondarily in the blue-violet regions of the spectrum.

[55] In a four-level system, the system insisted upon by Schawlow and other laser researchers, the brightness requirement for a laser-pumping lamp does depend on the crystal dimensions.

My calculations showed that I would have an adequate margin of safety, in terms of excess brightness intensity for the laser of, some two to three times, even with the smallest lamp, the FT-506 lamp.

Since the FT-506 required a lot less *total* energy and the crystal dimensions were not critical, I decided to concentrate the first design based on this lamp. But, to be on the safe side, I ordered and obtained several lamps of each size for backup.

## External Factors

In December 1959, Hughes announced that it was going to move its research laboratory from the Culver City Quonset hut to a new building that Hughes had leased in Malibu, California. Basically an empty shell, the building was located atop a mountain with a spectacular view of the Pacific Ocean.

Meanwhile, my wife and I were in escrow to buy a house in Palos Verdes. My daughter Sheri was an 18 months toddler at that time.

If we bought the house in Palos Verdes, it would be a 40 mile commute each way to the new Malibu laboratory. We backed out of the escrow and found a house in Pacific Palisades. Hughes generously paid the cancellation fee. I now had a manageable 10 mile one way commute.

For some time I had been doing a lot of my calculations and analyses at home. Shirley resented my homework. I can't say I blamed her for that, but it aggravated an already rocky marriage that terminated 10 years later.

The lab move was certainly not well timed for laser development. Coping with the problems of moving into a new house with a small child was distracting and dealing with a laboratory move to a new building, with non-operational facilities cost me at least three weeks of development time.

CHAPTER 11

# Let There Be "Coherent" Light

Based on my most current calculations and measurements, I was becoming optimistic about the possibility of creating a laser. The tension was building and I started to have dreams that I actually did it. It was a wildly exciting thought! If I really did make the first laser not only would I beat out some really tough, well funded competition, but also victory would be especially sweet since I would have succeeded by taking a path that had been shunned by the "hotshots" in my profession.

Still, I was worried that I might be missing something. Instead of proceeding directly to the actual design, I decided to do an experiment that would check the validity of my model.

I made-up a cube of pink ruby with each dimension equal to one centimeter in length, about the size and shape of a sugar cube. The crystal axis was perpendicular to one set of faces of the cube. I then placed the cube between two parallel plates, thus forming a microwave cavity. The cavity resonance was designed to be equal to the natural ground-state splitting of the ruby. These are the ground-state sublevels used in a ruby maser.

The purpose of this arrangement and the subsequent experiment was, to monitor the ground state population of the ruby. Remember,

Schawlow said that one wouldn't be able to substantially reduce the ruby ground state ion population necessary to make a laser. My calculations showed that it could be done but I wanted tangible evidence to confirm and justify my optimism.

I was still harassed by the thought: No one had yet ever made a laser, although by now, several *teams* of scientists had been diligently working away (with substantial funding, in some cases), for nearly two years in an attempt to do so. Was there a fundamental insurmountable problem I had missed?

On top of this, Peter Franken, a friend of mine and a well respected optical physicist, who was then a professor at the University of Michigan, planned to give an industrial course at the University in the summer of 1960. One of the course lectures was, "Why A Laser Is Not Feasible."

I kept returning to my model to look for any process that I hadn't considered, that could possibly defeat my concept. I did turn up of a couple of possible potential problems; certain conceivable energy level transitions that I wouldn't want.

Robert Satten, a UCLA professor and consultant to Hughes, is a theoretical physicist specializing in Crystal Field Theory. I asked Bob to check out my concerns. He made some elaborate calculations to check out the conceivable problems. At the conclusion, we decided that I was moving in the right direction.

I proceeded to go ahead with the experiment using the *ruby cube*. As described above, one set of parallel faces of the cube served as the resonant microwave cavity. I connected one of the open (second set of faces) of the cube to one end of a polished quartz rod called a light pipe. The other end of the light pipe was connected to an FT-506 flashlamp. The third set of faces of the cube was used to probe with selected wavelengths of light. I used the "loading" on the parallel-plate microwave cavity to monitor the ground state population of the ruby, making use of the microwave properties of ruby that I had learned from my work on a ruby maser.

When I flashed the FT-506 lamp, the cavity loading did indeed change. It decreased because, as expected, there were fewer chromium ions in the ground state. More important, *the magnitude* of the population change, 3 percent, was very close to the value I had predicted from my analysis of the experimental parameters. This was an extremely gratifying result since it gave further confirmation to my model and its analysis.[56]

Now I was getting more excited. Since I couldn't think of anything else to check, it was time to proceed with the definitive design of a laser.

## The Laser Design

My first thought was to use some modification of the elliptic-cylinder configuration that I considered for the mercury arc lamp as discussed in the previous chapter. The problem was, I would need a straight, rod shaped flashlamp, but the straight lamps in the catalogues that I checked didn't have high enough intensity. Therefore, I resorted to a different design and stuck with what was available—the spiral shaped lamps. I didn't want to get sidetracked at this time into the development of a special lamp.

I talked to one of the GE lamp distributors. He said that the FT-623 lamp was so bright that it would set a piece of steel wool that was placed close to it on fire.

It dawned on me that I would not have to devise a focusing arrangement at all. The brightness of the radiation that is attainable at the focus of a mirror or lens can only approach, but not exceed, the brightness of the source. This is a consequence of what scientists refer to as, *the second law of thermodynamics*.

So, why not just place the crystal in close proximity to the lamp. That is, why not place the crystal *inside* the lamp helix?

To help *gather* the light, I placed a polished aluminum cylinder around the outside of the spiral. To fit the lamp, I used a pink ruby crystal in the shape of a right circular cylinder rod, 3/8 inch in diameter by 3/4 inch long (about 1x2 cm.). The ends of the ruby cylinder were polished flat, parallel to each other and perpendicular to the axis of the cylinder. For mirrors, I used evaporated silver.

Ideally, I would want a high reflectance, thick opaque silver coating, at one end of the ruby rod and a partially-transmitting coating at the other end to extract the laser beam. These silver optical coatings are evaporated onto the crystal. A partially transmitting coating can be obtained by controlling the evaporation process to obtain a deposited thickness of somewhat less than one, one-millionth of an inch!

---

[56] The descriptions of these experiments were reported and published in *Physical Review Letters* 4, 564 (1960), under the title "Optical and Microwave-Optical Experiments in Ruby."

I chose silver for the mirrors because it has the highest reflectivity of any metal at the deep red ruby laser wavelength. However, silver tarnishes quickly. Consequently, with time, the thin output layer will change its transmission characteristics; it is not stable.[57]

To solve the silver tarnish problem, I had a *thick* layer of silver evaporated on *both* ends of the crystal and scraped a tiny hole in the coating at one end. The laser beam would emanate from that coupling hole.

The laser head was about the size and shape of a small water glass tumbler. That was the design. *Simple; aye?* (see drawing)

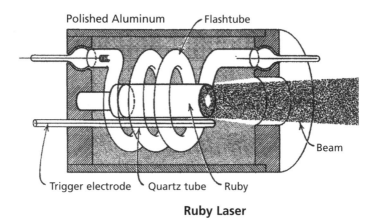

**Ruby Laser**

### The Crucial Test

As I neared completion in my laser design, Bob Hellwarth, one of my colleagues in the Atomic Physics department, asked, "How will you know if it's working?"

At first, I was concerned that if I were stuck with a ruby crystal that deviated too much from optical perfection, these imperfections could prevent measurable laser behavior.

To get a better understanding of the processes, I elaborated on my existing analysis to account for an imperfect crystal. I found that if I were able to drive the ruby crystal reasonably far above the point of inverted population, or laser threshold, that I would see very substantial evidence of an inverted population and impressive laser behavior even with a poor crystal.

---

[57] There was a new technology, called multilayer dielectric coatings, useful for high-efficiency optical mirrors, being developed in those days but that technology was not very far along.

Just exactly what would I see?

I planned to monitor the red light emitted from the ruby through the hole in the output silver coating and expected to observe three kinds of laser behavior evidence: A reduction in the decay time of the fluorescent level; the bunching of the radiation into a beam; and a significant reduction of the spectral width of the red light. These expectations and observations would result from a consideration of the following concepts.

## The Laser Process

Laser action can be understood by following through the operational details in the above-mentioned ruby laser design. The process starts when the ruby crystal is excited by the flashlamp and chromium ions are excited into the metastable fluorescent level. The ions lose energy by randomly radiating red photons. This is the familiar red fluorescence (spontaneous radiation).

When the excitation level is great enough, that revered inverted population condition is reached. In that case, more chromium ions are in the ruby's metastable upper fluorescent level than there are in the ground state. Therefore, chromium ions can radiate by *stimulated* emission (Einstein's *ser*), as well as by the normal spontaneous emission process.

Because the metastable level now empties much faster than it normally would, the fluorescent lifetime is reduced. That decreased lifetime can be observed by monitoring the red ruby glow with a photoelectric cell connected to an oscilloscope when the ruby is flashlamp-excited.

When the ruby is in the inverted population condition, as explained previously, it becomes an amplifier. The red photons are *amplified* as they progress through the crystal.

An important selection process starts to take place. The red photons are initially emitted in random directions. But the fluorescent photons that happen to be radiated at large angles to the mechanical axis of the ruby cylinder are lost through the sides of the crystal. On the other hand, photons radiated along the crystal axis, or at small angles with respect to the crystal axis, are in effect, trapped. They are reflected when they strike either one of the end mirrors and move back and forth through the crystal. As these axial photons move through the ruby they are amplified and consequently generate more photons in the same direction. They quickly become the dominant *stimulated* radiation from the excited metastable level.

Keep in mind, the photons moving through the crystal are responsible for the stimulated emission. The axial photons pick up a following and march down that crystal axis. Consequently, the photons that emerge from the coupling hole in the output silver mirror are concentrated in a direction along, or nearly along, the crystal axis.

The red ruby fluorescent (spontaneous) emission extends over a distribution of frequencies in a curve that resembles a bell shape. The fluorescent photons are most concentrated at the center of that curve. When the inverted population condition exists, the top of the curve has the highest amplification. The consequence is, (as with the discussion of beam angle) photons near the center of the distribution are favored, since it is these photons that get amplified the most in the back and forth transits, through the crystal from the multiple mirror reflections. It is this last process that explains why the frequency distribution, the *linewidth* of a laser is so small.

I planned to vary the excitation to the flashlamp. In doing so, as explained above, I would expect to see a reduction of the fluorescent lifetime giving evidence of stimulated emission. As I varied the ruby excitation level, the fluorescent intensity should increase proportionately, as long as I was below threshold. But, when above threshold, small increases in excitation should make much bigger changes in the output since the detector and monochromator combination are more responsive to the smaller beam angle and narrower linewidth.

I would be able to independently confirm the narrowing of the spectral width of the ruby's emission with an instrument designed specifically for this purpose, a spectrograph.

### Clogston's Proclamation

In April 1960, late in the development program, A.M. Clogston, Schawlow's boss at the Bell Telephone Laboratory in Murray Hill, New Jersey, visited the Hughes laboratory at Malibu.

Clogston commented, "We hear that you are still working on ruby." Apparently there was a leak from our lab in Malibu to Bell Labs. He went on to say, "We have thoroughly checked out ruby as a laser candidate. It's not workable. You will be wasting time, effort and money in a futile project if you continue."

More tension! Did Bell know something that I was missing?

## Do It!

It was the afternoon of May 16, 1960; it was time to confirm or deny all the fears of why the "ruby can't work"; Or, why "lasers can't be made to work." No more new calculations, no more diversionary experiments. This was the moment of truth!

The laser head was mounted on a workbench. The flashlamp was connected to the power supply. The trigger electrode was connected to the spark coil, (the mechanism that initiates the flash from the strobe lamp). The light output from the coupling hole in the end of the ruby was directed through the Bausch and Lomb monochromator to a photomultiplier tube, (a very sensitive form of photoelectric cell). The electrical signal from the photomultiplier was connected to a Hughes Memoscope.[58]

Irnee D'Haenens and I were the only ones performing and observing the experiment.

We first took a test shot so that we could adjust the monitoring equipment. We turned up the power supply to about 500 volts. We fired the flashtube. Indeed, we observed a trace on the Memoscope!

That trace was a recording of the red ruby fluorescence. The decay in the trace was about three milliseconds, the lifetime of the upper possible laser level. We made the appropriate adjustments to optimize the monitor display.

We continued. We progressively increased the supply voltage, each time monitoring and recording the light output trace. As we did so, the peak output increased proportionately to the energy input and the decay time remained the same … So far, so good.

*But, when we got past 950 volts on the power supply, everything changed! The output trace started to shoot up in peak intensity and the initial decay time rapidly decreased.*

*Voilà. This was it!*

## The laser was born!

---

[58] A special oscilloscope capable of retaining and storing flash signals.

CHAPTER 12

# The Light Fantastic

## The Hughes Reaction

When Irnee and I observed the first laser go into action, Irnee was smiling and jumping up and down with glee. I was numb and emotionally drained from all the tension and excitement.

The word spread quickly. Everybody came into our lab to see what we had. Bob Hellwarth was impressed and extended his congratulations. George Birnbaum was cool, not totally convinced.

Harold Lyons who had been concerned about the soundness of my concepts, and gave me a hard time about acquisition of the mono-chromator now got very got excited. The promoter in his soul saw some real public relations possibilities here.

Some backdrop. Months earlier, the position for Laboratory Head opened up at Hughes. Harold Lyons assumed and expected that he would get that position. He didn't, he was passed over in favor of the much younger Malcolm Currie.

Harold was furious and went into a sulk. He would come to work late in the morning and disappear into his office behind a closed door. He reappeared late in the day and went home.

When I got the laser going, Harold came alive; he was in my lab the next morning, May 17, at 9:00 a.m. He had decided that we should issue a news release. In principle, that was fine, but I had a lot to do before a news release would be practical.

## Crystal quality

Although the laser behaved as I had forecast and expected, the smooth rather than abrupt behavior of the threshold indicated a poor crystal quality. In order to demonstrate a more dramatic behavior of the laser, I put three new rubies on order from Linde Division of Union Carbide, the only supplier of man-made ruby material in North America.

The original ruby was cut from a raw *boule* purchased from Linde and fabricated by the Hughes machine shop. I was concerned about the quality of the Hughes shop fabrication, so when I ordered the new rubies I had them fabricated by Linde. I ordered three crystals so that I could have a choice of the best quality.[59]

## More Confirming Measurements

For purposes of publication and conviction to the outside world I wanted to make some additional measurements. Most important would be the spectral linewidth of the laser. A positive result would be very convincing confirmation of laser action.

In order to make that measurement I needed an expensive, highly specialized piece of equipment; a high-resolution spectrograph. By coincidence, such a spectrograph had just been delivered to Bob White's Solid State and Cryogenics section. But, there was a problem.

Ken Wickersheim, a scientist working for Bob White, had the spectrograph on order for at least six months and he had a number of experiments planned for his new equipment. Consequently, in no way was he inclined to move aside to let me use it.

I went to see Harold Lyons for override authority. Harold had stars in his eyes for the expected news release and so, much to Ken's dismay, Harold authorized my use of the spectrograph.

---

[59] The crystal growth engineer at Linde responsible for the manufacture of the original rubies was Ralph Hutcheson. Some years later, I got to know Ralph and we became good friends. He left Linde and founded his own company, Scientific Materials, which he has dedicated to the growth of high quality electro-optical crystals with emphasis on YAG (an explanation of this important laser crystal will be found later in the text).

I asked Charlie Asawa, one of the scientists in my group with expertise in spectrographic instrumentation, to assist me with the spectral linewidth data. With the aid of the spectrograph we were able to confirm that the laser output radiation showed the expected spectral narrowing. This was more exciting proof of laser action. The ruby, moreover, provided a built in reference control.

Ruby's red fluorescence actually consists of two very closely spaced spectral lines. They are referred to as $R_1$ and $R_2$. My analysis of the model showed that only one of these lines, the $R_1$ line, should lase. That is exactly what we found. The $R_2$ line did not narrow at all. When we operated *below* threshold, in the fluorescence mode, the spectral brightness of the $R_1$ line was only slightly greater than the $R_2$ line.

*But when we were above threshold, we observed a brightness ratio of more than 50 times; a further rock solid confirmation of laser action.*

Imagine: In the 10 years prior to the laser, the coherent electromagnetic had been extended by perhaps a factor of *five*. Now, with the advent of the laser, there was a quantum jump in that spectrum of *ten thousand*!

The significance of my historic accomplishment didn't sink in right away. I'm not sure that it has yet.

CHAPTER 13

# Publication Fiasco; Enter Politics

## Physical Review Letters Rejection

After I created the first laser and collected the data, I prepared a technical paper for publication. The proper journal for reporting my work should have been the prestigious physics journal *Physical Review*. Because of long advance publication times (four to eight months), Physical Review came out with an adjunct journal, *Physical Review Letters*.

The idea of *Physical Review Letters* was to provide a fairly fast publication time of some two to four weeks for breaking news. It was usual to write a brief description of new information and discoveries for publication in *Physical Review Letters*, followed later by a lengthy paper to provide more in-depth coverage of the subject for publication in *Physical Review*.

I sent a copy of my intended *Physical Review Letters* paper through the Hughes hierarchy for approval. The paper cleared this process, including a review by the Hughes Patent Department. The Patent Department cleared the paper without any delay. Strangely, Hughes didn't think that the report of my work was important enough for them to file for patent protection. As a result, Hughes lost any claim to foreign patent rights by allowing the publication and hence, public disclosure.[60]

I submitted my manuscript to Samuel A Goudsmit, the editor of *Physical Review* on June 22, 1960. Within just two days, on June 24, 1960, Goudsmit sent me a curt reply of rejection. In his rejection letter, Goudsmit stated that in the opinion of his referee, "It would be more appropriate to submit your manuscript for possible publication to an applied physics journal, where it would receive a more appreciative audience."

He returned my manuscript and enclosed an editorial he had previously published in *Physical Review Letters* along with the rejection letter. Goudsmit's editorial stated in effect, that *Physical Review Letters* was no longer interested in manuscripts discussing the merits of masers.

I had stumbled into a lose-lose situation! When I submitted my paper to *Physical Review*, I titled it, "Optical Maser Action in Ruby." But the term "optical maser," I insist, is an oxymoron.[61] Why would I use such a peculiar expression? *Especially, since what I was reporting on was no maser.*

I reluctantly did so because I knew the editorial staff at *Physical Review* were very stuffy and, if I had used the term *laser* that they may well have reacted negatively on the basis that, this was just some new "device" they had never heard of or that it was not a proper manuscript compared to the esoteric subjects that they favored in their publication. Since *Physical Review* had published the paper by Schawlow and Townes, which used that nonsensical optical-maser term, I thought I was safe.

*Given the nature of my paper, Goudsmit's reaction was astounding!*

Here was a major scientific breakthrough: A report of the creation of the first source of coherent light ever and the extension of the coherent electromagnetic spectrum by four orders of magnitude (10,000 times). But this information was considered *not worthy of publication in Physical Review Letters?*

I wrote back to Sam Goudsmit and suggested that, just perhaps, his reviewer had made a mistake. *Incredibly*, he fired back another editorial form letter in which he stated their policy: no manuscript once turned down, for whatever reason, could be reinstated. The reviewer's decision was final. What? The *Physical Review* and its referees are infallible?

---

[60] A full description of the Hughes patent department's unusual behavior and its consequences is forthcoming in Chapter 22.
[61] In Chapter 19 I explain why I say that.

The screening process at *Physical Review Letters* was obviously faulty. But once the momentous mistake was pointed out, the obstinate behavior of the editor was unforgivable.

Perhaps, you can imagine my *extreme* level of frustration. After successfully working through the reluctant Hughes sponsorship of my project, I proved the scientific community's prevailing wisdom incorrect. I was able to "scoop" well funded, powerful teams around the world who were attempting to find a viable laser concept. Now I couldn't get published?

This "comedy of errors" continued, although at the time the last thing on my mind was that these developments were funny.

## The Nature Publication

When I received the first rejection notice from *Physical Review Letters*, I prepared a shortened version of my paper and submitted it to the prestigious British journal, *Nature*, which was also known for relatively fast publication.

At the time of my appeal to Goudsmit to reconsider his decision, I disclosed my paper submission to *Nature*, but explained that I would withdraw the *Nature* paper if *Physical Review Letters* changed its mind and agreed to publish my manuscript. Goudsmit's response: "We don't duplicate publication."

The shorter version of my paper, which disclosed the first attainment of coherent light, was therefore published in *Nature* on August 6, 1960. The paper was titled, "Stimulated Optical Radiation in Ruby."

## Premature Public Release

While I was in the midst of arguing with *Physical Review Letters*, unfounded rumors surfaced that a laser was working, or nearly so, in some other laboratories. Hughes management was getting nervous. Here they had a public relations coup of a lifetime in their laps. If someone else had a news release first, a next day counter with "We had it working before you," wasn't going to wash.

I was determined to publish in a professional journal before any news was released to the public. But Hughes was so terrified about the possibility of being scooped that, over my strong objections, they proceeded with the news release. In retrospect, I'm amazed that I could have been so cool and confident to believe that the competition's efforts were not very close ... But, I was correct.

Goudsmit didn't react well to the news release, he said, "We don't publish material in our journal which has been released through the press." Of course a press release is a public, non-technical description, whereas the manuscript submitted to *Physical Review Letters* was highly technical for my peers. There should have been no conflict. Now, it became obvious, *Goudsmit was not going to publish my paper, no matter what.*

## Establishment Politics

My disastrous frustrating encounters with Samuel Goudsmit began a forty-year feud with the American Physical Society, the institution that publishes *Physical Review*. *I didn't fully appreciate it at the time, but I was bucking head-to-head with the well entrenched establishment, an old boy's club; an eastern clique of universities, Bell Labs and, some elite east coast research laboratories.* This establishment looks down upon industry in general, but they consider that the lowliest is the west coast aerospace industry (of which Hughes is an example).

It is interesting to note that papers *subsequent* to mine, on the same subject, were also submitted to the *Physical Review Letters*. These included papers from the Bell Labs report, which followed upon and *reproduced* my ruby work; the IBM report of Stevenson and Sorokin's uranium laser that adopted my flashtube concept; and Bell Lab's Javan, Bennett and Herriott report of their infrared gas laser. Their papers were all readily accepted and promptly published. These establishment authors didn't encounter any adverse editorials from Sam Goudsmit.

## One More Publication Goof

There was one more aspect to the publication fiasco. After failing to get published in the *Physical Review Letters*, I sent my original full manuscript to the *Journal of Applied Physics*. My paper was accepted, but the publication delay was six months.

At the press conference there were some preprints of the article that would appear in the *Journal of Applied Physics* on the table for the reporters. A week or two later, I received a letter from the editor of a publication that I wasn't even aware of: the *British Journal of Communications and Electronics*. *The editor informed me that he had published my Journal of Applied Physics preprint without my knowledge and permission!*

Understandably, the *Journal of Applied Physics* withdrew my paper from their publication.

CHAPTER 14

# The News Release

## Press Conference

Hughes was not the least bit shy about capitalizing on a great public relations opportunity. My department head, Harold Lyons, told me that he had experience dealing with the media and I did not. He said that he would personally take care of the news release; I needn't be present.

Mal Stitch who had previously had a falling out with Harold found out about Harold's news release intentions. Stitch "snitched" to Malcolm Currie, the current laboratory head. Currie, who generally didn't have a very positive view of Harold, immediately grasped the situation and ordered Harold to stay out of the news conference. I was scheduled to go in his stead.

Very quickly, an efficient sophisticated team was brought in; the Carl Byoir public relations agency was to handle the news release. Byoir handled Howard Hughes's personal public relations, and in 1960, was one of the top public relations agencies in the country.

A "hotshot" photographer showed up at my lab. He wanted me to pose for the key news release photos. In his career, he had very successfully placed photos of scientific devices. His "modus operandi" was to take a picture of the device held in front of a face.

So he had me pose with the first laser held in front of my face. He didn't like it, he said it was too small, not good proportions. He looked around the lab and spotted one of my backup laser designs (the middle size FT-503 flashtube), which he thought might be more appropriate. Is this a laser? Yes. I held it up in front of my face and he loved it. But, I was very disturbed. "Wait a second," I said, "that's *not* the *first laser, this is!*" He replied, "Look, this is what's called 'creative license.' You do the science, I do the pictures. If it bothers you that much, hold your hand on your stomach to stave off the nausea."

He took some other pictures of apparatus in the lab that had little or no connection to the laser. He said he needed a few extra pictures to "stuff " the press kit, but that 90 percent of the story pickups would use the picture of my face with the, *not the first laser.*

He was right!

The Carl Byoir executive assigned to handle the release was Bill Utley; he was a real pro. First, he argued, Malibu, California is not going to get much attention. We need to find an excuse to have the release in New York City. I'm not sure how he pulled it off but, indeed, on July 7th 1960, a press conference was held at the Delmonico Hotel in New York City. The turnout was impressive. The *New York Times, Time* and *Life* magazines, *Newsweek, Christian Science Monitor,* all the major press agencies were represented. The pressroom was filled. The release itself is duplicated below:

From:Carl Byoir & Associates, Inc.          FOR RELEASE AT
     c/o HUGHES AIRCRAFT COMPANY          11 A.M., EDST, THURSDAY,
     Florence Ave. & Teale St.          JULY 7, 1960
     Culver City, Cal.
(UPton 07111, exts. 2423 & 2149)

U. S. VICTOR IN
WORLD QUEST OF
COHERENT LIGHT

Hughes Scientist Reveals Man's First
     Creation of Long-Sought Source
        'Brighter Than Sun's Center'

NEW YORK, July 7 -- Man for the first time has created a source of "coherent" light—"an 'atomic radio-light' brighter than the center of the sun"—a scientist of Hughes Aircraft Company, Culver City, Cal., announced at a press conference in the Delmonico hotel here today.

Dr. Theodore H. Maiman showed for the inspection of newsmen a "laser" (from Light Amplification by Stimulated Emission of Radiation), a new solid-state electronic device, smaller than a water tumbler and containing a synthetic ruby as its "heart," which he said is being used in the company's research laboratories to generate the coherent beam.

"Achievement of the laser (sometimes called an optical maser) by Hughes marks the culmination by American industrial research of efforts by teams of scientists in many of the world's leading laboratories, some private and some publicly supported, some working under defense contracts and some not," Dr. Maiman declared, "At Hughes the work was done with the company's own funds."

500, 000 Billion Cycles

"As a scientific advance the laser projects the radio spectrum into a range 10,000 times higher," he said. "The radio spectrum is the range of electromagnetic frequencies starting with commercial radio at one million cycles per second and extending into the upper microwave region of 50,000 million cycles. The laser jumps the gap from 50,000 million cycles to 500,000 billion cycles, opening the way for a host of important applications."

He cited:

1. True amplification of light (for the first time in scientific history).

2. A new scientific tool for investigating properties of matter and performing basic experiments of physics.

3. Focusing of light into high-intensity beams for space communications.

4. Vast increases in the number of available communications channels.

5. Utilization of high light concentration for industrial, chemical and medical purposes.

How Laser Works

Dr. Maiman said he has described the laser in a paper submitted to the Journal of Applied Physics. The essential steps in its operation are simple, at least from the scientist's point of view, he said. He listed them:

1. A light source, such as a powerful flash tube lamp, irradiates a synthetic ruby crystal.

2. The optical energy excites the atoms to a higher energy state from which the energy is reradiated in a narrow band of frequencies.

3. The excited atoms are coupled to an atomic resonator and stimulated to emit the radiation together, hence the acronym laser. This is in contrast to ordinary light sources where the atoms radiate individually at random and is responsible for the incoherence of these latter light sources.

Atomic Radio-Light

Dr. Maiman said that the laser could be described as an "atomic radio-light" because its coherent properties are similar to radio waves and it uses atomic methods to generate light beams "brighter than those of the sun or stars, even at their hottest centers."

He said the laser could be used as a "light radar" to direct light waves, rather than radio waves or microwaves, to a target, even in outer space. Reflected back, these waves would provide a "picture" of super-clarity never before attainable, he added.

For use in TV and voice communications, the needle-sharp light beam provides a secure "private line" free from static and resists, deliberate "jamming," Dr. Maiman said.

"The laser's use in radar and communications for space work is obvious since there is no atmosphere in space to absorb or scatter the beams," he said, "The high resolution resulting from its sharp beams would enable man to take detailed 'pictures' of any area. For example, a beam directed at the earth from a satellite 1,000 miles up could be concentrated in an area about 200 feet wide."

Declaring that lasers could generate "the purest colors known," Dr. Maiman explained that in principle light waves could be produced more than a million times monochromatic (single-hued) as those from a mercury or neon lamp.

### Concentrates Beam

The laser generates an almost perfectly parallel beam, spreading only a slight amount, he said. For example, the laser can generate a beam less than a hundredth of a degree of arc wide which, when reaching the moon nearly a quarter million miles away, would illuminate a lunar area less than 10 miles wide. By contrast, he said, if a search-light (of ordinary light) could reach the moon, its beam would spread over 25,000 miles because it is a finite-sized incoherent source and the brightness is correspondingly reduced.

"When light energy is concentrated in such small areas as it can be using a laser, the beam's illumination intensity is very great and it therefore could generate intense local heat," he said.

"This suggests the possibility of many uses such as sterilizing surfaces with the laser's beam, which can be focused to a needlepoint," he added, "Perhaps individual parts of bacteria, small plants and particles could be vaporized. Surface areas may be modified when the laser beam's light and heat induce chemical or metallurgical changes. This could be useful in biology, medicine and industry."

### Additional Information

Dr. Maiman said the laser beam could be sent, for example, from Los Angeles to San Francisco, without spreading more than 100 feet, while a searchlight beam would spread about 50 miles.

The laser emits the sharp coherent light beam in the extremely high frequencies of optics—about 500,000 billion cycles per second—where electromagnetic waves become light, he said. In the optical region, the distance between crests of a wave is 27 millionths of an inch as contrasted with the microwave region where the wavelength is about one inch or radio waves where the length is 300 yards, he explained.

Therefore, laser beams can be concentrated to a pinpoint size approximately 27 millionths of an inch in diameter, he said.

"The word 'pinpoint' is apt," he said, "because the head of a pin is two million times larger in cross-sectional area than that of the focused beam."

To generate a light wave as intense as that produced by a laser, a carbon-arc Hollywood klieg light theoretically would have to reach a temperature of several billions of degrees (the surface of the sun is 6,000 degrees Centigrade)—a purely hypothetical example since the lamp's materials would disintegrate if such heat could be achieved, he said.

Dr. Maiman explained that the word "temperature" as applied to the laser is not the common conception of the word, but rather is a temperature equivalent to that which an ordinary light source would need to generate a signal as bright as the laser's at the laser color. This is why the laser unit itself does not "burn up," he said.

7/7/60-0-

## A plumber's kit

The Hughes and Carl Byoir entourage arrived at the hotel the night before the press conference. The head of Hughes Public Relations, Bob Meyer, was in our party. He asked to see the laser since I had brought it along to the news conference. When he saw it he was aghast. "My God," he said. "We're in big trouble!" "Why?" I asked.

"You mean that this is what all the fuss of this release is about? *It looks like something a plumber made!*" I thought it was rather simple and elegant looking.

At the press conference I made a presentation. I tried to explain the significance of the scientific breakthrough, *coherent light for the first time ever.* Because of its unique and useful properties, the laser would spawn a host of applications, including its use as a scientific tool in many different disciplines from medicine and biology to chemistry and physics. It would, in all likelihood, be used for high information-bandwidth communications and, most certainly in industry, to drill, cut and weld. I didn't foresee the supermarket checkout scanner or the laser printer.

## Time-Life

The press conference was extraordinarily successful. Not only was there a turnout of every major news organization with global coverage, but also the attention at the meeting was deafening. The discussion as well as the question and answer period went extremely well. Then, there were some fireworks. Jack Jonathan, the science writer for *Time & Life* magazines, was seated at one of the front tables. Jonathan suddenly picked up his press kit and slammed it down on the table. He yelled, "*What kind of hoax is Hughes trying to pull here?*"

There was silence for a moment. Seated opposite Jonathan across the front table was Sir William Lawrence, science writer for the *New York Times.* Bill Lawrence tried patiently to explain to Jonathan the nature and significance of the laser development. Jonathan only became angrier and turned red in the face.

After the press conference, Bill Utley took me to Jack Jonathan's office in an attempt to soothe his feathers. Jonathan sat at his desk with his arms folded. He was very stubborn; he said he would wait for confirmation from another laboratory.

### Death Ray

When I stepped down from the podium after the presentation and the Questions & Answer session at the press conference, reporters immediately surrounded me. A reporter from the *Chicago Tribune* took the lead and said, "We hear that this laser is going to be a weapon." I replied that he wouldn't have seen anything like that in the press kit. "Well, but what about it?" I answered that I would put such usage well down on a list of practical uses and, if it did come to pass, that I would expect it to take at least twenty years. He persisted and asked the same question in several different ways. Finally he tried, "Well, Dr. Maiman, are you willing to say that the laser could *not* be used as a weapon?"

"No, of course not, I can't say that, but …" I began.

"That's all I wanted to know," he said and cut me off. Being a novice at interaction with the media, I was startled and shaken by that dialogue.

The next day, there were front page stories in all the major United States papers, such as the *New York Times, Chicago Tribune, Los Angeles Times* and many newspapers outside the United States. Major news magazines covered the story in their next news cycle.

Many of the newspaper stories were headlines. The *Los Angeles Herald's* headline was red and two inches high. All of the story headings were some variation of:

*"LA Man Discovers Science Fiction Death Ray!"*

That's how the laser was introduced to the world.

### Bette Davis

The Death Ray label took a number of years to shake off. When I would meet new people in a social situation and the laser came into the conversation, the reaction was almost always "Oh, you mean that Death Ray?"

One particularly noteworthy event occurred when I was at a party and was introduced to actress Bette Davis. I was one of her fans and excited to meet her, so I was really taken aback when she asked, "How do you feel about being responsible for that death and destruction?" I defensively stammered without an answer.

But, to her credit, Miss Davis made a point of finding me before she left the party. She said, "I've been thinking about what I said to you and I was unfair. I think it is up to the scientists to develop new technology and up to society to decide how to use it."

## The Life and Death Ray

I was being interviewed on a radio broadcast when the interviewer asked the same question:

How I felt about creating a "Death Ray." This time I did not stammer and said, "The term Death Ray as applied to the laser is a misnomer. I don't know of anybody who has been killed by a laser, even accidentally, but I do know of some people who have been healed by a laser." By now, the laser had been used successfully to repair detached retinas.

The interviewer quickly changed the subject. Thereafter, I reversed my defensive stance on the Death Ray.

I could tell the public mood had changed when I would meet new people and I might hear for example, "Thank you for saving my grandmother's eyes."

Weapon lasers *have* been made over the years. But they are huge monstrosities with severe practical limitations. For sure, they are not of the *Flash Gordon* or *Star Wars* variety.

Lasers however, *are* extremely effective when they are used for precision guidance of *other weapons*. Well known, of course, are the "smart bombs" that were used in the Gulf War and Vietnam; but, at least as far as I know, no Death Rays yet.

At the same time, lasers have become an unqualified success in a myriad of medical applications.

*In reality, the laser is more of a Life Ray, not a Death Ray.*

CHAPTER 15

# Aftershocks and Ripple Effects

## Pandemonium

As a consequence of the wide coverage received by the Hughes news release, pandemonium broke out. I received letters, telegrams and telephone calls from all over the world. Some callers were very creative. The manager of the Ice Capades called me to express an interest in the laser because it radiated a *pure* color. He wanted to use it for spotlights!

The owner of Knott's Berry Farm thought the laser would make a good ray gun to shoot at wooden ducks (it does). The president of the American Meat Packer's Association had me on the telephone for an hour; he wanted to use the laser to stun hogs.

Government contracting agencies called to *give* Hughes contracts for laser research and development; they were especially interested in classified military applications.

Now, *Physical Review Letters* had their ultimate excuse to cover their colossal goof in the treatment of my paper. They were not going to print something in their highbrow technical journal after a public release of the information. I admit (as I had requested to Hughes) that I would rather have had Hughes wait until I had resolved the publication problems. On the other hand, the *Physical Review* editors who were so indignant about the news release were using it as an excuse to cover their blunder of having dumped my paper.

Six months later, Bell Labs had a public news release on their helium-neon gas laser, also *prior* to publication in *Physical Review Letters*. In this case, there was no problem from the editor of that publication. There are different rules for members of the establishment.

## Trauma at Bell

By the time of creation of the ruby laser at Hughes, Bell Telephone Laboratories had invested millions into the programs of Sanders, Javan and Schawlow. They had expected to be the winners in the laser race. One of the most prestigious laboratories in the world with almost unlimited resources and a house full of top level scientists had committed itself to developing the first laser. *They didn't.*

*Worse*, the heart of the first laser was a *pink ruby crystal*. Bell had gone on record damning the use of pink ruby for a laser, saying it couldn't work. It was Schawlow, in his remarks at the first Quantum Electronics Conference and in his paper on the published proceedings, who in effect condemned the pink ruby. Also, just three months earlier, Clogston (Schawlow's boss) had declared, in a private comment during a visit to Hughes, *"work toward a ruby laser is a waste of time."*

I particularly remember and savor a phone call that I received from my friend Peter Franken in the aftermath of the news release. He called to congratulate me and said that what he especially enjoyed was the fact that I had beaten out Bell Labs. The Bell Labs' arrogance was well known and not appreciated.

There were many very fine scientists working at Bell Laboratories. In the subsequent years, a significant number of the important advances in laser technology did indeed, come forth from this world-class laboratory. They can be very proud of their contributions.

*But ... on July 7, 1960, Bell Telephone Laboratories was not enjoying a good day. They seem not yet to have recovered from that startling and dis-comforting news; They still have the spin going.*

## The Science Community Reaction

The scientific community was stunned. The Hughes news release had caught everybody off guard. The expectation had been that when the laser appeared on the scene it would be some form of gas or vapor device and, that it would emanate from Bell Labs, Columbia, TRG, or some other laboratory where there was a major funding effort. Certainly, it *would not* be a solid-state laser, which used the condemned pink ruby crystal.

The stuffier part of the science community (the establishment) was in shock and indignation that they were first informed of the news via a sensational newspaper story. They expected that when the laser breakthrough emerged, the first report would be found in a respected physics journal with peer review.[62] As indicated above, they too used the newspaper route when it suited their purpose.

The trade press was having a problem. They too, knew that there were well motivated efforts in a number of highly respected laboratories to realize coherent light. They also, fully expected that when success was achieved, it would be in the form of some kind of gas laser and that the accomplishment would most probably emanate from Bell Labs or the Columbia Radiation Laboratory. Or, perhaps, it would come from MIT's Lincoln Laboratory, from IBM, GE, or TRG, but certainly not from some unknown at the Hughes Research Laboratory.

Naturally, the laser would not be based on the use of a ruby crystal.

So, there was a little confusion for a while. The press was not sure whether what I accomplished was real or not. One trade magazine, to cover itself, titled its coverage *"If he has what he thinks he has, he has a laser!"*

Ironically, in a surprising turnaround, within a few days after the Hughes announcement, Arthur Schawlow conceded that he was persuaded my ruby laser was, in all likelihood, working!

But, not so, Schawlow's co-author and brother-in-law, Townes.

## The Townes Reaction

In 1960, Charles Townes was vice president of a small prestigious government agency, The Institute for Defense Analysis (IDA). IDA informed Hughes that it wanted to hear a presentation of my work.

Hughes had been reluctantly digging into its own pocket to fund my project, my work was *not* government funded. Consequently, Hughes did not have to comply. Still, Hughes did depend heavily on government contract funding and was concerned that it would not be politically correct to turn down the IDA request.

---

[62] If I had not had the publishing problem with the editor of *Physical Review Letters*, the first report of coherent light would, indeed, have come from the pages of a technical journal.

Harold Lyons and George Birnbaum, both friends of Charles Townes, gave me my marching orders to Washington D.C., IDA headquarters. An Air Force colonel, the contract officer for TRG's contract with ARPA, was also present at the meeting. The million-dollar ARPA-funded TRG contract was based on Gordon Gould's laser concepts and proposals. It was now also an ARPA embarrassment that TRG was beaten out.

I found myself in a very hostile environment. Townes carefully listened to my presentation but he was unreceptive to the suggestion that I had a working laser. *He argued that I must have been observing some kind of artifact!*

I was taken aback. This was an astonishing comment when considering *all* the phenomena that I had observed: the super-linear behavior of the output; the large decrease in decay time of the spectral output; and the tremendous narrowing of the spectral line. The "clincher", of course, was the built in *control* behavior of the non-lasing $R_2$ line.

What do I mean by a built in control? As pointed out earlier, the ruby lased only on the $R_1$ line and not on the $R_2$ line. Based on the model I had set up, this was as expected. Since these two fluorescent components are so similar in all aspects within the crystal, heating or other peculiar non-lasing effects would have shown up in both lines. It's a bit like a double blind medication trial. In this case the $R_2$ line was, indeed that control.

The weight of the evidence was overwhelming, *this was no artifact*. On the contrary, the sensible conclusion was that I had achieved a laser.

## The stark contrast

Could it be that Charles Townes was shaken and embarrassed that he and his Columbia team had not pulled off the hapless potassium-pumped-potassium vapor laser that he and Art Schawlow had featured in their *Physical Review* paper?

The fact that my ruby laser couldn't have been more *drastically different* than what Schawlow and Townes had proposed in their paper must have been very troubling indeed.

(1) A small, room temperature, solid ruby crystal is nothing like a hot potassium vapor-cell.
(2) An emission wavelength in the visible red is 4½ times higher in the electromagnetic spectrum than the Schawlow-Townes prognosticated infrared frequency.

(3) An output power of many kilowatts was more than one million times greater than their expected power level of one milliwatt.

## Denial

The TRG contract officer was visibly relieved that Townes had come to a negative conclusion regarding my laser. He said, " I'll continue to bet on our horse."

The colonel's relief was short lived. Townes and the colonel were in stunned denial.

## New "Stubby" Rubies

On July 20, about two weeks after the Hughes news release, I finally received the three fabricated and polished rubies from the Linde division of Union Carbide that had been on order for the last two months.

These new Linde rubies were the same chromium concentration as the original ruby. They were exactly the same ⅜-inch by ¾-inch (approximately 1x2 cm.) size as the original ruby. Charles Townes, in his autobiography, derisively refers to this particular ruby shape and size as a "stubby ruby."

As I had hoped, these three new rubies did have better quality than the original one. I popped the first specimen from the new batch into the laser head and replaced the original.

## Then … kaboom!

When we turned up the power supply this time, we found a very sharply defined threshold and we saw a small brilliant spot on the wall. Even the doubters and naysayers couldn't deny my ruby laser anymore. The other two Linde fabricated (stubby) rubies also worked beautifully.

## Laser Research and Funding Explosion

The news of the laser's creation stimulated a veritable explosion of funds for laser projects. Scientists who were already working toward lasers altered their courses and redirected their work. Others, who had not previously worked on any laser project, now joined in. At Bell Labs, a *red* team of six scientists was assembled.[63] This group of six studied my news release and scrutinized the picture of the *not the first*

---

[63] R.J. Collins; D.F. Nelson; A.L. Schawlow; W. Bond; C.G.B. Garrett; and W. Kaiser.

*laser* depicted in the release. The picture showed an FT-503/524 flashlamp and a ¼ by 2 inches long ruby.

About six weeks later, the group of six succeeded in getting a similar ruby laser going. Not surprisingly, their laser configuration *consisted of a long narrow ruby in an FT-503/524 flashtube just as shown in the newspaper photo.*

## Bell Labs' Dirty Tricks

In late August, R.J. Collins, one of the group of six at Bell Labs, called me at Hughes, to ask for the specifics of my laser publication in the British journal, *Nature.* I responded to his request and gave him the reference. I also used the opportunity to tell him that any controversy over my ruby laser could now and forever put to rest. I described to him the dramatic July 20 performance of the laser when the Linde fabricated rubies were inserted into the laser head. Collins stammered: "I've been told not to discuss scientific information over the phone."

*Why not?*

When publishing scientific papers, it is usual ethical practice and standard procedure to disclose such information as a footnote on private communication and to acknowledge the source.

Bell Labs had no trouble in getting their submission accepted in the *Physical Review Letters.* They didn't have a rejection from the editor, Goudsmit. They wrote and published a paper about "their" ruby laser and its dramatic performance.

*They made no mention in their paper of the information that I had conveyed to Collins on the phone.*

## Ken Wickersheim

One of the repercussions of the news release aftermath had an amusing twist. At Hughes, when physicist Ken Wickersheim was prevented from using the high resolution Bausch and Lomb spectrograph that he had waited six months for, he was understandably frustrated and annoyed. Ken impatiently waited for Charlie Asawa and I to finish our spectral measurements on the laser using *his* spectrograph. Finally, in disgust and dismay, he gave up. Ken decided to go on vacation to get away from the laser that he now loathed with a passion.

Ken headed for the hills, literally; he went backpacking in the California mountains. On July 8, 1960, as he climbed up to the top of a mountainous trail, he came to a small convenience store in the middle of nowhere. There on a newspaper displayed on the stand outside of the store, Ken read the newspaper headline:

"LA Man Discovers Science Fiction Death-Ray"

Induction into the Royal College of Surgeons of England as the only non-physician, non-royal member of the society.

In Israel receiving the Wolf Prize. Erwin Hahn is pictured on the right.

Kathleen and I having some fun in the Greek Islands, just after receiving the Wolf Prize.

In Argentina, hours before the attempted kidnapping, with John Carruth and Masha and Isaac Kaplan. John and Isaac are laser physician pioneers.

With Kathleen and prominent laser physicians Peter Asher, Richard Dwyer and Mahmood Mirhoseini

The Fortieth 'Ruby' Anniversary of the Laser's Birth
was held May 16, 2000 at the Terminal City Club,
Vancouver, Canada

In an overwhelming show of support, colleagues and friends
travelled from far and wide to attend. (Photo by Arlen Flax)

With physical chemist Ricardo Pastor, and laser physicists Don Devor, Irnee D'Haenens and Vicktor Evtuhov at our home.

With my Stanford thesis professor, Nobel Laureate Willis Lamb

Kathleen and I dancing at the anniversary party

Dr. Hans Rottenkolber, myself and Willis Lamb.

Professor Wilhelm Waidelich, Germany's pioneering authority in the physics of laser medicine, and his wife, urologist Dr. Raphaela Waidelich.

In Germany, September 2000, recovering from laser surgery, with Dr. Hofstetter, world renowned laser urologist, and Dr. Raphaela Waidelich, my personal urologist.

A recent photograph with my wife Kathleen, on a cruise in Mexico.

CHAPTER 16

# Nullification Tactics

The old boy "establishment" had a difficult time coping with the traumatic blow that I had dealt them by both, beating them at their own game and, in a manner that they had publicly declared as not practically possible. Fortunately, I had not followed the teachings and prognostications of Schawlow and Townes and, in their eyes this was a mortal sin.

Many instances of questionable tactics used by the establishment to manifest their displeasure were demonstrated over the years. They could not make me go away, but they did find ways to "sweep me under the carpet." They had the power.

I did receive some awards sanctioned by the American Physical Society (APS) as they couldn't afford to ignore me entirely. However, the award committees "watered-down" their citations of the world's first laser by describing it as "The first pulsed-laser using a ruby crystal", or, "The first solid-state laser." These are *technically* true statements, but the implications are certainly misleading.

Would you report the accomplishment of the Wright brothers with the citation: "For the first flight with a biplane that used wing warping for guidance"?

*Or* ... "For the first manned flight".

When I was granted awards free of the influence and pressure of the power structure at the APS, they were "pure." That is, they always said, *for the first laser*, as for example, when I received my Japan Prize.

## The Twenty fifth

Early in 1985, I was contacted by some of the organizers of a joint APS and IEEE[64] meeting, to honor the laser's twenty fifth anniversary to confirm the exact birthday of the laser. I gave them the information, that is, May 16, 1985. Accordingly, the meeting was set during that week and, subsequently, every year, the meeting continues to be on that date.

In an astonishing move, the organizers of the conference did not follow through by inviting me to be the featured speaker. When colleagues heard that I was not only not the featured speaker, but also not even an invited speaker on the program, a huge cry of protest was registered. Consequently, a belated invitation for me to speak was reluctantly offered.

Considering the circumstances, I declined.

## The Phony Fortieth

After already admitting that May 16, 1985 was the 25th birthday of the laser, the establishment attempted to revise history. In 1998 Bell Labs, together with Schawlow and Townes, had a big party celebration in San Francisco declaring the 40th anniversary of the laser. They asserted that the publication of the Schawlow-Townes 1958 *Physical Review* paper (in December, 1958)[65] constituted the birth of the laser. ...What?[66]

*Not only was there no laser in 1958; but, no one has yet sighted a Schawlow-Townes laser.*

## The APS Timeline

Recently the American Physical Society set up a web site with a recitation of important technological developments of the twentieth century. I was contacted to submit a picture of the first laser. I submitted the picture, but was aghast when I saw the context in which it was put. I was listed under Construction of the Laser. The maser was listed with credit to Townes for Laser Development.

---

[64] The Institute of Electrical and Electronic Engineers.
[65] Please read Chapter 19.
[66] The meeting, as noted above, was held in May. How did they explain that??

*Where is the laser that Townes developed??*

The APS presentation is, of course, incorrect. As of this writing, the web site on the APS timeline continues to be as I have described it and yes, Charles Townes is a past president of the APS.

Independent media, whose articles are researched by competent science reporters, have no difficulty in presenting the information correctly. Twentieth century technology time-lines were published in *Time* Magazine and *Business Week* during early 1999. In marked contrast to the APS rendition, both of those time-lines cite the birth of the laser in 1960 with credit to T.H. Maiman. Neither Schawlow nor Townes is even mentioned.

An especially egregious example of nullification methods is documented below.

## The Berkeley Conference

The Second International Conference on Quantum Electronics was held in Berkeley, California on March 23-25, 1961. This was the sequel to the 1959 Shawanga Lodge Conference discussed in Chapter Nine.

At the 1959 Shawanga conference, a number of laser papers had been presented in *proposal* form. No workable details or calculations were given, no viable laser concept was on the table. Remember, at the 1959 conference Schawlow himself said, "As yet, nobody knows for sure what form a practical source of coherent infrared or optical radiation will take."

The theme of the first Q.E. conference at Shawanga was the hope, … the dream, that someday it would be possible to generate coherent light. *Between the times of the two conferences, it actually happened!* Not in any of the forms envisaged at that conference, but it did occur and it initiated, a veritable explosion in the scientific, industrial and military regimes.

The whole theme of the Berkeley conference should have been, *It's here! It really can be done.* Let's savor this moment. Let's celebrate. How can we make more, better and different lasers? Now that coherent light exists, how can we make use of its wonderful unique qualities?

## The Berkeley Conference Program Game

I recently had the occasion to peruse through the published proceedings of that second Q.E. conference. In the introduction/prologue the only reference to the astonishing change in status between the two conferences was the lame comment, "These possibilities are primarily due to our newly developed coherent light sources which are a major topic of this volume."

The seven page conference introduction is peppered with name-dropping, I counted 32. However, the name Maiman was conspicuously absent.

The author of the prologue references Charles Townes five times, yet the person responsible for the night and day difference between this conference and the last one is not acknowledged in that prologue.

It gets worse. The first section of the conference was, indeed devoted to lasers. They had twelve such papers scheduled. They couldn't obliterate me and were obliged to include me to speak at the conference. But there were ways and means to play around with the schedule.

Charles Townes presented the first paper. He had the opportunity to set the tone of the conference. But, Townes made no reference to the dramatic breakthrough that had taken place since the last conference ...

Instead, he went off into the blue beyond with proposed esoteric applications for the laser. Curiously, my name was not spoken in the body of the Townes paper or in his printed references at the end.

The second paper was co-authored by Townes and four other scientists at the Columbia Radiation Laboratory[67] That paper discussed the *failed* $2\frac{1}{2}$ year alkali vapor project.

Townes' former student, Ali Javan, gave the third paper covering his co-development with W. R. Bennett, Jr. and D. R. Herriott of the fourth laser.

W.R. Bennett Jr., another Townes student, presented the fourth paper ... and so on.

The twelfth paper, the last one, was mine. That was the paper that reported the creation of the world's first laser!—and, my name does not start with "Z."

---

[67] H.Z. Cummins, I. Abella, O.S. Heavens, N. Knable, and C.H. Townes

CHAPTER 17

# Bandwagoning

## Presence

There is an interesting juxtaposition of reality and human nature that the historical writers often do not take into account. You might call it the *presence* effect.

When scientists are working toward a never-before attainable goal, they seldom admit it, but there are always nagging doubts hanging over their heads. Can it really be done? Is there some physics we're neglecting? What fundamental or practical limitations might prevent it from ever becoming a reality?

In other words, the sought after goal doesn't yet exist. More important, it may *never* exist. It is *not present.*

This thinking puts a distinct damper on funding for the science venture in question. It keeps other scientists away from the project, not only because of the lack of funding, but the risk of failure. People are hesitant to work on a possibly "go nowhere" project; except of course, for the inveterate risk takers.

When success does arrive, there is a tremendous change in mood, outlook and motivation. Hey, it really does work! It *can* be done.

*Now, all of a sudden, it looks easy.* It should have been done years ago. Oh, I had that idea first. He must have gotten the idea from me. It was an accident, he just *stumbled* on it.

Once you show them how, then everybody can do it and is doing so.

It is *now present.*

In a lecture at the Sorbonne, Albert Einstein said, "If my theory of relativity is proven successful, Germany will claim me as a German and France will declare that I am a citizen of the world. Should my theory prove untrue, France will say that I am a German and Germany will declare that I am a Jew."

So, it was with the laser. Hughes, who had so reluctantly and begrudgingly funded my laser development with, "You're wasting our precious General Research Funds, go work on something important, like computers," now had a news release proclaiming the wonderful breakthrough that came from the Hughes Research Laboratories.

## Copycat Lasers and other Laboratory Curiosities

Armed with the information and accompanying picture in the Hughes news release, increasingly laser researchers found it irresistible to pop a favorite crystal into an FT-503/524 flashlamp to see if they could get laser action. A series of "copycat" lasers quickly emerged.

Inspired by the success of the ruby laser, Mirek J. Stevenson and Peter P. Sorokin, scientists who worked together at the IBM Thomas J. Watson Research Center, set about to make a four-level solid-state laser. They adopted the ruby laser pulsed flashlamp approach and succeeded in making a crystal of calcium fluoride *doped* with uranium lase in late November 1960. Their laser operated at 2.5 microns, a spectral wavelength in the infrared that is about three and a half times lower in the spectrum than the ruby laser.

The uranium laser requires less pumping power than ruby because it operates at an infrared wavelength and is, indeed, a four-level system. But, it becomes four-level only when it is cooled cryogenically. As pointed out before, the power to the flashlamp can be lower in a four-level system but this benefit is outweighed in a cryogenically cooled version of a four-level laser by the enormous energy requirement to reach and retain cryogenic temperatures.

Early in 1961, there were two more cryogenically cooled flashlamp-pumped crystal lasers: Stevenson and Sorokin's samarium-doped calcium fluoride and Schawlow's dark ruby satellite-line laser.

As previously noted, Schawlow, at Bell Labs, had tried in vain to make his dark-ruby, four-level laser work and abandoned it.[68] From the Hughes news release, the information was now available on just how to make crystal lasers work. Simultaneously, Irv Wieder and Lynn Sarles at Varian Associates, and Schawlow and Devlin at Bell Labs, were able to make the dark ruby lase, when they cooled it with liquid helium and pumped it with an FT-503/524 flashlamp.

Schawlow and many other early laser scientists were so obsessed with the idea of the inherent superiority of a four-level system, compared to a three-level system that, again, they didn't bother to make the calculations and take into account all of the other pertinent considerations.

I have steadfastly maintained that cryogenics is a device killer. Indeed, the 1960 crystal lasers which followed after ruby turned out to be mere laboratory curiosities which quickly vanished.

*Despite its much maligned, three-level nature, the ruby laser reined as king of high power lasers for more than ten years.*

## More Presence Effect

The presence effect could not be more aptly demonstrated than by the following example, where William R. Bennett Jr, a Bell Labs scientist who worked with Ali Javan and Donald Herriott on Bell's gas laser, tells in an interview with *Science* magazine:[69]

*"An atmosphere of skepticism about laser oscillators pervaded Bell Laboratories before Maiman's announcement. At one point, the Bell administration considered cutting off funds for research on the helium-neon laser, just months before it was made to work. It was only after Maiman demonstrated that a laser actually could be built that the clouds of skepticism lifted. Then money quickly became available for all kinds of laser projects."*

After the Hughes news release communicated the existence of the first laser, Javan's project suddenly received much attention at Bell. Now knowing that a laser could be made, Bell heavily pushed the development. As a result, the team of Javan, Bennett and Herriott, in late December 1960, were able to make an operational continuous gas-discharge laser. Their laser used a mixture of helium and neon gases and operated at a wavelength of, 1.1 microns, in the invisible infrared.

Since you can't *see* this infrared wavelength, and photographic film and photomultiplier tubes can only marginally detect it, this laser had

---

[68] Schawlow's interview in, Laser Pioneer Interviews, *High Tech Publications, Inc.* December 1985, page 59.
[69] Science, Vol. 216. 23 April 1982.

very limited use. Consequently, like the cryogenic crystal lasers, Javan's 1.1micron gas laser was destined to join the group of laboratory curiosities.

In fact, the vast majority, of the hundreds of lasers discovered through the years, have been relegated to the laboratory curiosity shelves. Once written up in a scientific journal, they too disappeared.

Nearly two years later, in 1962, after Javan had left Bell Labs, White & Rigden, two other Bell Laboratory scientists, devised a way to make a *visible* red helium-neon gas laser. They used gas pressures and ratios different from the original Javan laser, a drastically smaller vessel cross-section (important) and a different set of energy levels. The red helium-neon laser of White and Rigden became very successful and was widely used for many years. Recently the diode-semiconductor lasers have largely replaced it.

## Laser Efficiency

Intuitively, one might think that gas lasers would be more efficient than crystal lasers. Why? Because gas lasers get excitation energy directly from an electrical input, they would seem to be very efficient. Crystal lasers on the other hand, use a two-step process. First, there is an electrical input to the flashlamp or other optical pump lamp. Second, the incoherent radiation from that pump lamp energizes the laser crystal.

In practice, the opposite is the case. Gas lasers tend to have efficiencies of only about one tenth of one percent or less. That's *one part in a thousand* and is typical of the helium-neon laser as well as the argon and krypton ion lasers.

As I pointed out earlier, the processes in a gas discharge are very complex. There is much competition among numerous transitions. As a consequence, only a tiny fraction of the electrical input energy ends up in the desired laser transitions. By contrast, crystal lasers have efficiencies of one to five percent; that is ten to one hundred times more efficient than a gas laser.

## A Continuous Ruby Laser

In 1965, Evtuhov and Neeland successfully designed and operated a room temperature *continuous* ruby laser at Hughes. The design they used was essentially the AH6 elliptic cylinder design that I had worked out in 1960 but neglected to build because of the marginal calculated operation.

As I have explained, at the time that I worked on the original development, no laser had ever been made, *so there was no presence effect then.* By 1965, not only was the laser present, but also there was *ruby laser presence* and much data had been gathered on ruby. Consequently, an intelligent choice of specific design parameters could be made. Evtuhov and Neeland did an excellent job of doing just that.

Just as I had calculated and worried about it, the operation of the AH6 design was indeed marginal.[70]

---

[70] D.F. Nelson and W.S. Boyle made a continuous ruby laser in 1962 but it required cryogenic cooling and hence joined the array of laboratory curiosities.

CHAPTER 18

# Forty Years of Spin

When the creation of the ruby laser was announced, Schawlow and Townes, with the help of the gigantic Bell Laboratories public relations machine, went into immediate damage control. Their spin activities have continued unabated over a 40-year span, even into an attempt to revise history, as described previously in Chapter 16.

Art Schawlow proclaimed that he had first *mentioned* ruby and Maiman "implemented" it. That is an astonishing comment considering that at the Shawanga Conference, he *condemned* the pink ruby and said it wasn't a workable laser. In so doing, he mislead the laser community.

Validation of the 1958 Schawlow-Townes *Physical Review* proposal paper was proclaimed. They alleged that my laser was "a result of, and flowed directly from, the principles and teachings of their publication. I merely implemented their ideas."

Absurd of course, but a good shot at spin and damage control. *Not only did I not follow the Schawlow-Townes teachings but rather pursued a course counter to their directions.*

The centerpiece of the 1958 *Physical Review* publication was the potassium-pumped-potassium infrared laser proposal. As noted previously, Charles Townes had headed a Columbia Radiation Laboratory team of five scientists[71] in a well funded, highly motivated quest for a laser. By the time of my announcement in July 1960, they had worked for nearly two years on their mission, but the project had not been a success; *nor was it ever a success.*

Bell Telephone Laboratories sponsored several parallel laser efforts with multimillion-dollar combined expenditure of funds. These efforts included the one spearheaded by Art Schawlow, as well as those of Sanders, Javan and others.

A million dollars had been put into TRG laser projects by funding through ARPA.

There were also many other parallel laser efforts in the United States and around the globe.

Since the Schawlow-Townes paper had been published and widely circulated in the scientific community, all of the above named projects had full access to that paper, its purported teachings and principles. Yet, with that knowledge, *none were able to produce a laser.*

As John F. Kennedy once said, "Failure is a bastard but success has a thousand fathers."

## Some Sour Grapes

The Hughes news release of the first laser created havoc in some quarters of the scientific community. There was the excitement, of course, but also a ripple of sour grapes. "He stumbled on it by accident!" "It's only pulsed!" "It only uses three-levels; four would be better."

By far the wildest story that I heard floating around was, "Maiman worked at Bell Labs where the laser idea was hatched and Hughes paid him to steal the idea!" *What?*

Of course, I had never worked at Bell Labs, *however, my father had,* seventeen years earlier, when I was 16.

An interesting coincidence is that my father Abe worked at the Bell Telephone's Murray Hill Laboratory at the same time that Charles Townes was there. They worked on the same radar bombsight project and had desks down the hall from each other.

To digress for a moment I would like to relate an early experience. Around March 1, 1956, shortly after joining the Hughes Research

---

[71] Townes, Cummins, Abella, Heavens and Knable.

Laboratory, I attended my first professional meeting in Asbury Park, New Jersey called, Symposium on Amplification by Atomic and Molecular Resonance. The United States Army Signal Corps was the symposium sponsor.

At that meeting, Charles Townes made a presentation in which he discussed his ammonia maser. A competing professor in the audience from MIT, MWP Strandberg, stood up and said "Well, there is nothing special about the ammonia maser, one could make a maser out of just about anything: *even including the right mixture of Vodka and Old Crow.*"

My father had taught me that science is an ethical and respectable profession. Scientists deal with each other in a gentlemanly fair way. So, I was taken aback at that mocking remark from a respectable scientist and felt sympathetic for its victim, Townes. But, as I found out later, science can get nasty and Townes is no victim.

In 1985, in a published interview, Townes stated: *"I didn't really expect making lasers to be as easy as it turned out to be."* Later in the same interview, when asked about my ruby work, he responded: *"Almost everything works if you hit it hard enough".*[72] These are curious remarks from someone who headed a team of scientists in an intense, but *unsuccessful,* effort to achieve the laser.

But, what is more interesting is the illustration that "what comes around goes around."

### Internet Spin

If you peruse the Internet, you will encounter more spin by Bell Labs, claims that Bell Labs "invented the laser".[73] It's easy to cut through that kind of spin with a few obvious questions:

(1) Where is the picture of the laser that Bell Labs invented??
(2) If Bell Labs had invented the laser wouldn't they have made the first laser? Even the Bell website begrudgingly acknowledges— with faint praise—that the first laser was my creation.
(3) Was Bell Labs not highly motivated to make the first laser?
(4) Was Bell deficient in financial resources?
(5) Did Bell not have the high-power scientists in place?

---

[72] Laser Pioneer Interviews, *High Tech Publications,* December 1985, page 41 & 42.
[73] The patent "showcased" on the website is the "paper patent" discussed in Chapter 23. It is explained in that Chapter how it is possible to obtain a patent for a concept that doesn't work.

## The Grape is Still Sour

In 1995, Donald Nelson who was head of the group of six Bell Lab scientists that was able to *reproduce* my ruby laser after they read the Hughes news release, wrote a letter to the editor of *Laser Focus* magazine that can only be described as bizarre. In that letter, Nelson alleged that I could not have created a laser because I didn't use a *rod-like* shape for the ruby and I didn't report *spiking*[74] behavior. He said that a stubby ruby couldn't work.

Since I reported the detailed measurements on the short ruby in several publications, including a 1961 *Physical Review* paper reviewed by Townes,[75] I don't know what Nelson could have been thinking!

What boggles the mind is the fact that the *rod-like* shape, used by Bell when they reproduced my work, was derived from the newspaper picture that accompanied the Hughes news release. In his letter to *Laser Focus* magazine, Nelson readily admits that the Bell work was stimulated by the news release. What is amusing is that the picture of the *not-the-first-laser* clearly shows a rod-like structure.

*The rod-like configuration was also my original design.*

In the same vein, not long ago, Townes wrote me a letter. He stated that Nelson made a calculation that showed that the short ruby couldn't work, but I need not worry, Townes wouldn't publish that revelation.

I don't know who should be more embarrassed, Nelson for making the erroneous calculation or Townes, for not checking it himself and repeating Nelson's fallacy.[76]

Apparently to this day, after forty years, Townes and Nelson remain in a state of denial ... *that the stubby ruby works.*

---

[74] An erratic sub-pulsing observed in the output of some lasers.
[75] T.H. Maiman, R.H. Hoskins, I.J. D'Haenens, C.K. Asawa and V. Evtuhov, Stimulated Optical Emission in Fluorescent Solids Part II, Spectroscopy and Stimulated Emission in Ruby, *Physical Review*, 123, 1151-1157 (1961).
[76] Before going into publication of this manuscript, I hooked up the original laser, which I still retain. Of course, as always, I used a non rod-like "stubby ruby" (about 9x18mm). That laser still works. It meets the Townes criteria of a red spot on the wall. It meets the Nelson specification of "spiking behavior". *And, even meets the Maiman demand of effortlessly boring a hole in a Gillette razor blade!*

CHAPTER 19

# Exploding a Myth

In prior chapters I have referenced a *Physical Review* article authored by Schawlow and Townes. Their paper was written in August of 1958 and distributed widely within the scientific community prior to publication in December 1958. It was titled "Infrared and Optical Masers"[77] This paper has been described by some as, a "seminal" paper in the history of lasers. That's not a consensus. I am amongst those that take a different view.

I would like to introduce a critique of the aforementioned publication because it illustrates to the reader a style of science subscribed to and used by, some, but certainly not all scientists. The Schawlow-Townes publication offers no proofs nor is there experimental data offered to show validation of the concepts presented.

By contrast, it is the style of most scientists to make measurements and validate their concepts before they publish their work.

A more appropriate title for the Schawlow-Townes paper would have used the word *proposal*. Scientists who write such a paper are, in my opinion, trying to stake out a claim.

It is my contention that the paper did not present notable new ideas and certainly not, any workable solutions. On the contrary, there were a number of very vague suggestions presented together with one

---

[77] Infrared and Optical Masers, *Physical Review*, Vol. 112, 6, December 15, 1958.

preferred specific proposal that was, as will be explained, mortally flawed.

### Reinvention of the Fabry-Perot

A dominant theme in the publication was an analysis of the modal behavior of an optical resonator. The authors' approach to the problem was to start with considerations of microwave structures and then evolve into the optical domain. This is not a surprising revelation since microwave spectroscopy was a strong part of the background of these authors. They had jointly written a book on that subject.

After some lengthy reasoning, Schawlow-Townes arrived at their proposed optical resonator. It would be a structure with two parallel end plates and open sides. This configuration, however, was not new or novel.[78] It was well known to optical physicists for many years since *C. Fabry and A. Perot invented it in 1899!* Accordingly, this resonator is in fact, called a *Fabry-Perot* resonator.

To me, it seemed rather obvious to at least consider the Fabry-Perot as an early choice to begin with. If you're going to work in the optical part of the spectrum, why not consider first what's already there?

It is certainly true, that when scientists well versed in one discipline shift their field of interest and become engaged in another discipline that they often bring new principles, ideas and thinking to the transferred field. This concept has been aptly demonstrated many times in the field of lasers where much analytical thinking and technology from electronics was infused into the field of optics. Nevertheless, it also doesn't make sense to, in effect, "re-invent the wheel."

The fact that R.H. Dicke at Princeton University in 1956 proposed the use of a Fabry-Perot, as did Gordon Gould in his laser patent application, further supports my argument that the Fabry-Perot resonator was an obvious choice as part of a device to generate coherent light. Gould and Dicke both easily arrived at the use of a Fabry-Perot without the laborious reasoning of Schawlow-Townes.[79] *In my opinion, it would be hard to make a case for not using a Fabry-Perot.*

The concept of using any resonator to couple to the laser medium also was not novel. Any one grounded in electronics knows that the most

---

[78] I used a parallel-plate microwave resonator in my doctoral thesis experiment at Stanford.

[79] The definitive analysis of optical resonators didn't evolve until *after* the inception of the laser. It was Fox and Li in 1961 and, Boyd and Kogelnik in 1962, who most notably contributed to that understanding. Both groups worked out of Bell Labs.

basic oscillator configuration is an amplifier with a gain of one, a tuned circuit (resonator) and positive feedback. Besides, as noted previously it was Fabricant who suggested the use of a resonator in conjunction with an active medium to form a laser many years earlier.

## The Deficient Potassium Vapor Proposal

A key feature of the Schawlow-Townes paper was a specific proposal and method devised to generate coherent infrared radiation at a wavelength of 3.14 microns. This wavelength corresponds to an electromagnetic frequency five times lower than visible light.

They planned to construct a quartz cylindrical cell about 10 centimeters (4 inches) long and one centimeter in diameter. The cell would be filled with the vapor from the basic chemical element potassium. The cell would be placed between two external mirrors to form a Fabry-Perot resonator.

One of these external mirrors would be partially transparent and the hoped for infrared beam would be extracted from that mirror. The cell would be placed in an oven at a temperature of 325 degrees Fahrenheit to get the vapor pressure of the potassium up to the desired level.

Schawlow and Townes proposed irradiating the potassium vapor-cell with the light from a potassium-containing electrical discharge lamp. The purpose in so doing was to energize the atoms in the potassium vapor-cell and produce the crucial inverted population necessary to realize an infrared oscillator.

Without scrutinizing the details, Schawlow-Townes assumed that they could take advantage of what is referred to as *resonance absorption.* They argued that there would be a match between the discharge lamp and the vapor-cell since the same chemical element (potassium) is in both with the same energy level structure.

Schawlow and Townes calculated that they needed vapor-cell absorption of 1.2 milliwatts. As a model light source they considered a commercially available potassium discharge lamp made by Osram. *Even when the lamp was overdriven to three times its design value, the measured power available at the desired wavelength was only 0.4 milliwatts,* too small by a factor of three.

It is not feasible to transfer all of the radiated power from the potassium lamp to the vapor-cell because of reflection losses and inefficiencies of mirrors and/or lenses. A transfer efficiency of perhaps fifty percent, at most, might be realistic. That factor was not put in their calculations. Just from their own considerations presented so far, the anticipated shortfall in pumping power is at least a factor of six.

Further, when we consider other details not discussed in the Schawlow-Townes paper, we come to a different conclusion completely. The assumption of a match between the very low-pressure vapor-cell and a much higher-pressure discharge lamp, even though they both employ the same chemical element potassium, is a very naive concept.

The emission or absorption of radiation from a collection of atoms is not all exactly at one precise frequency, but rather takes place over a finite range of frequencies. The parameter that characterizes that phenomenon is referred to as the *spectral linewidth* of the atomic transition in question. The minimum width of an atomic transition is determined by the spontaneous emission rate—the inverse of the lifetime of the upper level. In any normal circumstance, a number of different factors contribute to the broadening of a spectral line, over and above that limiting value caused by spontaneous radiation.

In a low-pressure gas, such as the potassium vapor in the vapor-cell mentioned in the proposal, the dominant cause of spectral linewidth is the movement of the atoms from thermal energy; that is, from the finite temperature of the gas—just like the familiar random movement of air molecules. The consequent contribution to the linewidth from this effect is called *Doppler* broadening. It is a similar circumstance to the change in pitch that you perceive when listening to a train whistle as the train goes by.

The conditions in the potassium discharge lamp are totally different. First, the temperature in the discharge lamp is higher than the temperature in the potassium vapor-cell. Accordingly, there is a larger Doppler broadening of the lamp output radiation compared to the Doppler broadening of the vapor-cell absorption line.

Second, the vapor pressure of potassium in the discharge lamp is some 10,000 times higher than the gas pressure in the vapor-cell. Consequently, the interactions between the atoms themselves (collisions) as well as interactions between the atoms and the walls of the discharge tube are, in this circumstance, important. This result from this effect is called *pressure* broadening.

Third, unlike the low-pressure vapor-cell, the discharge lamp has electrons and potassium ions within its envelope to maintain the discharge. The electric fields from these charged particles give rise to an effect known as *Stark* broadening.

*Taking these factors fully into account indicates that the spectral width of the lamp is apt to be some 10 to 30 times greater than the linewidth of the absorption cell. The lamp and the cell do not match!*

Since the energy of the lamp radiation is spread out over a large bandwidth, the comparatively narrow linewidth vapor-cell can only absorb a small fraction of the potassium lamp radiation.

Considering all of the above, I concluded that the proposed potassium-pumped-potassium infrared laser design was deficient in pump power by a factor of one hundred!

Omission of the spectral analysis of the pump-lamp versus the vapor-cell is a fundamental deficiency of major consequences in the Schawlow-Townes paper.

### "Has to Work"

In a published interview in *Laser Pioneer Interviews*,[80] and also in his autobiography, Charles Townes proclaims: "My style of physics has always been to think through a problem theoretically, analyze it and then, do an experiment which *has* to work. You analyze and duplicate the theoretical conditions in the laboratory until you beat the problem into submission, you see."

It's been my experience, that when you are working on something new, science can provide surprises. Some of your assumptions may be incorrect. There may be parameters that you failed to include. There may be unexpected unknowns, like the effects of unavoidable impurities. It's hard for me to imagine an experiment in a *pioneer* area that *has* to work.

Townes headed the team of scientists at the Columbia Radiation Laboratory that strived for the potassium-pumped-potassium system for more than two years … *It did not work.*

It is my belief that failure of the potassium vapor proposal was due primarily to the problems I enumerated above and secondarily, due to impurity problems from high-temperature potassium corrosion.

---

[80] Laser Pioneer Interviews, *High Tech Publications,* December 1985, p41.

## Staking out a Claim

To further ensure a stake in their *Physical Review* paper, Schawlow and Townes used a clever ploy. Since Townes was correctly known for his development of the first working maser, they titled their paper "Infrared and Optical *Masers.*"

The term, "optical maser" is an *oxymoron.* Townes had already defined the acronym *maser* to stand for **m***icrowave* **a***mplification by* **s***timulated* **e***mission of* **r***adiation.* Light and microwaves lie in two very different parts of the electromagnetic spectrum separated by a factor of 10,000.

The physics, implementation and instrumentation of lasers are totally different and distinct from that of masers. The maser turned out to be an ineffectual technology as discussed in previous chapters. In contrast, lasers are found everywhere.

Townes and the Bell Labs contingent (the establishment) stuck to their "optical maser" designation until Townes got his Nobel Prize. Then they gave up because the rest of the scientific community refused to go along with that name and insisted instead, on the term laser.

The Schawlow-Townes proposal, however, was a very successful scientific public relations coup, even though the paper did not teach one how to solve the laser problem. Their use of the term optical maser, together with wide circulation of preprints of their *Physical Review* paper, successfully served the purpose of staking out a claim.

They did succeed in causing some confusion about who did what. Regrettably, even in science, public relations and spin control can be effective in the promotion of a gross misconception.

CHAPTER 20

# Exit Hughes, Enter Korad

## Hughes Departure

In December 1959, I submitted an unsolicited proposal to the Air Force Laboratory at Wright Field, Ohio, to develop the ruby laser. A contract award based on this proposal did not come through, at least not right away. The contract award did appear immediately after the July 7, 1960 news release.

Under that contract, I continued to refine my measurements on the ruby laser. I reported the dramatic behavior of the Linde-fabricated (stubby) rubies in my first monthly report under the contract on August 1, 1960. I also reported the latest information at the October meeting of the American Optical Society that same year.

Late in 1960, Harold Lyons left Hughes to become vice president of Electro-Optical Systems in Pasadena, California. George Birnbaum was promoted to replace Lyons as head of the Atomic Physics department. I was promoted to section head of Quantum Physics.

Bela Lengyel also left and became a physics professor at Northridge College in the San Fernando Valley area of Los Angeles. There he wrote a book on laser physics. He sent me an autographed copy of his book with the inscription: "To Ted Maiman, who made the first laser, from Bela Lengyel, who wrote the first book about it."

In the aftermath of the ruby development, a company wide feeding frenzy started. Different divisions of Hughes were vying for control of the laser. I was feeling restless at being pulled into the political mire of the Research Laboratory and I didn't have a pleasant relationship with George Birnbaum, who was now department head.

I started to look around and consider the possibility of moving to another company. The interviews were a bit discouraging though; what I perceived at other places was a similar cast of characters, just different names.

Early in 1961, I received a telephone call from an ex-Hughes employee, Leonard Pincus. Len wanted to know if I might be interested in coming to work for a new company called Quantatron. My first response was *"What* is Quantatron?"

Quantatron was a newly formed company financed through venture capital funds. I interviewed at Quantatron and received an offer for the position of vice-president of the Applied Physics Laboratory. As I thought about it, the idea of being a big frog in a small pond became appealing. I announced to Hughes that I would leave the research laboratory in April 1961. My announcement triggered action on the company's part. Hughes immediately decided to file for patent protection on the laser.[81]

## Holding onto the Historic First Laser

On the day that I left Hughes, George Birnbaum followed me around as I picked up personal belongings from my office and lab. George handed me the original laser and said: "Here, you might want this." I said, "Thank you, I would like to keep it." That is how I came to have the historic world's first laser in my possession.

When I was at the Hughes Malibu laboratory, I had made up three slightly modified and improved versions of the first laser for further experimental work. Some years later, Hughes gave one of those modified copies to the Smithsonian Institution.[82] The second modified laser copy was given to Charlie Asawa when he retired from Hughes. Hughes themselves kept the third modified copy of the first laser at their laboratory in Malibu.

I have heard that they wished they had retained the original, so they wouldn't have been stuck in demonstrations with a copy!

---

[81] More on the Hughes patent story in Chapter 22.
[82] The Smithsonian, knowing full well that they merely have a copy, have pursued me to donate the original laser to them.

## Growing Ruby Crystals

When I set up the Applied Physics Laboratory at Quantatron, I hired some other departing Hughes personnel for specific purposes. There were a total of eight of us who left Hughes for Quantatron. Hughes was not happy about it, but working conditions there had deteriorated to the point that Hughes was very vulnerable to employee loss and it was easy to recruit people from them.

One of the new activities that we set up at Quantatron was the in-house growth of ruby crystals. The only North American supplier of man-made ruby at that time was the Linde division of Union Carbide.

A Frenchman, Verneuil, invented the basic process for the growth of these crystals. He taught the Swiss how to do it. The Swiss for many years used this technology to make the jewel bearings in their famous precision watches. They made their tiny jewels out of red ruby instead of clear crystalline alumina (aluminum oxide) because the clear water-white crystals were too easy to lose during the assembly of the watches.

During World War II, the United States government convinced the Swiss to transfer their technology know-how to the Allies, since it was needed for critical military use. Union Carbide's Linde division was chosen to receive the technology transfer. After the war Linde used the technology know-how to build a profitable business making synthetic gems. The synthetic gems had better optical properties than the natural gemstone but not as good as needed for top quality laser crystals.

Ricardo Pastor, a physical chemist and a veritable materials genius, was one of the key people who came to Quantatron with me from Hughes. Rick and his brother Tony set about to devise methods to grow laser-quality ruby.

The Verneuil process consists of starting with alumina powder with the appropriate doping with chromium oxide in the case of making ruby, placing it in a hopper and, with the aid of an automatic small tapper, causing the powder to impinge on a seed crystal.

The seed crystal is then mounted on a pedestal with the tip of the crystal heated by a very hot torch able to keep the tip of the crystal molten. Ruby melts at 2,200 degrees Celsius. As the powder falls through the flame it melts and builds up more crystalline material on the starter seed.

As the crystal grows in size, the pedestal is slowly lowered to keep up with the new growth. It takes about eight hours to grow a crystal 3 to 4 inches long by about 3/8th inch diameter.

Rick studied the process, and determined that the water content of the powder had an important effect on its flow properties, and that even tiny amounts of impurities could have a significant effect on the crystal growth and the quality of the ruby end product.

He developed methods to make ultra-high purity powder with precisely controlled water content. Tony re-engineered the burner and powder handling process. The result from application of these advanced methods to the growth of Verneuil rubies was a significant improvement in laser quality. These Quantatron and the subsequent Korad ruby crystals were clearly superior to the Verneuil crystals from the synthetic gem source at Linde.

## Korad

Quantatron was a subsidiary of Union Texas Natural Gas Company. Venture capital monies had funded Quantatron, but the assets were not well managed and the funds were rapidly dissipated. Early in 1962, Allied Chemical Company acquired Union Texas.

By now, I had built up my laboratory to 35 people. Allied Chemical was not too interested in funding my laser development work, so I scouted around for possible solutions to this new dilemma.

I found a very interested party in Union Carbide Corporation. I negotiated a deal with them and they (Union Carbide) bought my lab from Allied Chemical.

We incorporated my laboratory into a new company, which I named KORAD from Coherent Radiation with the 'C' hardened to a 'K'. I was named President of Korad. The company was funded and majority owned by Union Carbide. Key employees owned the remaining stock. Union Carbide had options to purchase the minority employee stock interest over five years.

Serving as chief executive of a small new company was an interesting and challenging experience for me. Union Carbide provided generous funding as promised in our negotiated contract.

Initially, the Korad revenue stream came largely from United States government contracts. But Union Carbide encouraged and induced us to gradually phase out the government support and work toward the establishment of a commercial product company and that's what we did.

## The Q-Switched Laser

The heart of the Korad product line was a series of very high-powered ruby lasers. The most popular and successful products were the *giant pulse* or Q-Switched lasers. Let me explain.

Late in 1960, Bob Hellwarth, a colleague and theoretical physicist in the Atomic Physics Department at Hughes, had a brilliant idea. Let's backtrack, to understand his concept:

When a pulsed crystal laser is constructed, the power-supply charges and puts energy into a capacitor bank. The capacitor stores this energy until the flashtube is fired and the stored energy discharges through the tube, giving rise to the brilliant flash. That is what happens when the electronic flash is fired in a camera. The only difference is that the camera gets its primary energy from a battery instead of a power supply.

The laser crystal absorbs the bright light from the flash and the active ions are raised to their excited levels allowing the amplification to rapidly build up in the crystal. The laser light is emitted from one of the semitransparent end mirrors.

Bob Hellwarth's concept was to temporarily block the build up of the laser oscillations by isolating the back mirror with an electro-optical switch in the laser cavity until all of the energy is stored in the excited fluorescent level of the ruby, at the upper laser level. The block is then very rapidly removed electronically. The gain in the crystal is so high that the oscillation builds up at an extremely rapid rate and, very briefly, rises to an enormous intensity. The result is a laser output pulse with huge peak power that lasts for a tiny period of time.

As an example, a particular ruby laser may emit a peak pulse power of say 10 kilowatts that lasts for 2 milliseconds in its normal operating mode. But, in the giant pulse mode, the pulse length might only last just 10 nanoseconds (billionths of a second) with a peak power intensity of 100 megawatts (100 million watts) instead of 10 kilowatts!

The generation of such huge peak powers is of enormous consequence as a scientific tool. It is also useful in a wide range of practical applications that encompass laser range finders (optical RADAR) and flash holography, which is a form of three-dimensional photography.

The Korad Company consistently supplied the highest power lasers compared to its competitors throughout its corporate history.

Several years after the development of the laser, Bob Hellwarth left Hughes to become professor of Electrical Engineering at the University of Southern California. He has continued through the years to distinguish himself as a prolific and highly productive scientist.

Bela Lengyel and I jointly served successfully as expert witnesses for Bob Hellwarth in the Q-Switch patent interference between Hellwarth and Gordon Gould.

### The Magic of Non-linear Optics

The huge peak power available from Q-switched lasers makes some normally rare physical phenomena turn into practical reality. The effect that I'm referring to is called *non-linear optics*.

When light of ordinary intensity interacts with optical materials like glass or transparent crystals, except for some reflection and/or refraction, the light passes through essentially unaltered. But when the intensity level is raised sufficiently, things change.

It is very much like the behavior of your stereo high-fi system. The amplifier behaves in a *linear* fashion at low levels and faithfully reproduces the music content. However, if you turn up the volume too high, you will start to hear *distortion*. The stereo system doesn't sound as good at these high levels because the over-driven amplifier adds new frequencies that were not present in the original music.

Essentially the same thing happens when very high-power light propagates through optical materials. These materials go non-linear and produce frequencies (wavelengths) that were not present in the original light.

The main exploitation of non-linear optical effects is the production of *harmonics*. These are frequencies that can be any multiple of the original light frequency.

So, for example, if we send infrared light from a Neodymium doped YAG[83] laser through a non-linear crystal, then magically, green light comes out. Or, if we pass the red light from a ruby laser through certain non-linear crystals, we get ultraviolet light out.

---

[83] YAG stands for "**yttrium aluminum garnet.**" Neodymium is one of the "rare earth" chemical elements. Neodymium-YAG lasers emit infrared light.

The consequence is that the very easy to pump YAG laser which normally can only produce infrared, can now readily produce visible green light. Also, ultraviolet, which is very difficult to produce directly, is available via non-linear optics.

Peter Franken and associates witnessed the first observation of optical harmonics in 1961 when they directed the red beam from a Q-switched ruby laser through a quartz crystal and thereby generated ultraviolet light.

It was Nicolas Bloembergen who developed the definitive analysis of the complexities of non-linear optics. For this work, as well as his fundamental work on the solid-state maser, Bloembergen received a Nobel Prize in 1981.

## Prokhorov

During the Korad years I had a number of interesting encounters with the Russian physicist and Nobel Laureate Alexander M. Prokhorov.[84] On one of these occasions, Prokhorov was on a visit to the United States to attend an international professional conference on lasers and electro-optics. He was in Southern California and had hoped to visit the Hughes Research Laboratory in Malibu. This was at the time of the Cold War and Hughes refused to admit Prokhorov even into the lobby of their facility. I thought that the Hughes action was unduly harsh and an insult to an internationally known and admired scientist. It would have been easy to escort him on a brief tour where there was no sensitive material to be seen.

When I heard about the Hughes action I extended an invitation to Professor Prokhorov to visit Korad. I personally escorted him through "innocent" areas of our plant. He vowed that he would reciprocate and invite me to visit the Soviet Union. I was disappointed that he never did.

A couple of years later, I planned to attend an international laser meeting in Paris. Before I left on my trip I was contacted by the United States Central Intelligence Agency. The CIA knew that scientists from all over the world, including those from behind the Iron Curtain, would be at that conference. I was enlisted to keep my eyes and ears open to gain any possible insight as to the status of laser technology on the other side.

---

[84] As previously noted, Professor Prokhorov is one of the three scientists who received a Nobel Prize for development of the ammonia maser.

At the Paris meeting, I met Professor Prokhorov again. He has a very charming way about him and was very friendly. He asked me many questions. I needed to be very careful in my answers. When I asked him reciprocal questions, he became extremely evasive. He told me that all the work I asked about was being done elsewhere in the Soviet Union. He proclaimed that he was unfamiliar with that work and had no knowledge of it.

That night, the Russian delegation hosted a dinner party for conference attendees. I didn't attend, but I heard that the Vodka flowed generously and as a result there were some loose tongues.

I didn't turn out to be a very good spy. I had little to report when I returned to the United States and was debriefed by the CIA.

## ИНСТИТУТ ОБЩЕЙ ФИЗИКИ

117942 Москва, ул. Вавилова, 38.

Телефон: 135-82-96
Для телеграмм: Москва В-333, ИОФАН

ACADEMY OF SCIENCES OF THE USSR

## GENERAL PHYSICS INSTITUTE

117942 Moscow, Vavilov street, 38

Telephone: 135-82-96
Cables: Moscow B-333, IOFAN

```
Prof. T.H.Maiman
13900 Tahiti Way
Marina del Rey
California 90291
USA
```

Dear Professor Mainman,

I was very glad to receive your kind letter of August 16 reminding me of our previous meetings many years ago which I greatly enjoyed.

It was a pleasant supprise to me to know about your second discovery that we share the same birthday. I take this opportunity to wish you health and success in the coming New Year and hope for future meetings.

Sincerely yours,

A.M. Prokhorov

CHAPTER 21

# A Solution Looking
# for a Problem

## Early Hype

Laser hype quickly outpaced reality in the early post laser era through most of the 60s. It was easy to see that, in principle, the laser promised much. The potential was clearly there but the progression was slow at first.

I attended an IEEE (Institute of Electrical and Electronic Engineers) meeting in the early 60s. One of the speakers at the conference made the statement: "The laser promises much but doesn't come through; the laser is just a *'solution looking for a problem.'* I was annoyed at that comment since it came across as a sarcastic put down of the laser. After further thought I decided that the *laser was a solution looking for a problem.* But I was thinking in a positive way.

I was convinced that the unique properties of lasers would, in time make them useful to solve many problems. Yes, time was needed to develop uses for the laser since it was a totally new tool.

Peter Franken visited me in Los Angeles around then and taking me aside, he said: "OK, Ted, just between you and me, do you really think the laser will ever amount to anything?"

"*Yes*, be patient Peter," I said hopefully.

Soon after, the editor of one of the trade magazines interviewed me at Korad. He needled me about the gap between the laser hype and fulfillment. Never mind that he himself belonged to the group who wrote all that hype in the expectation those sensational stories would boost readership.

The trade editor tried to provoke me further. "Dr. Maiman, *do you think that a laser will ever be practical enough to be used in anyone's home?"*

I pondered, "I don't know why not!" although at that moment, I didn't have any specific idea in mind.

His question and my answer stuck in my mind. They came back to me many years later when I presented a lecture at a hospital facility whose staff had recently been trained to use lasers in many different surgical applications. A physician in the audience commented to me that it had occurred to him that *he had six lasers in his home.* He listed two CD players, a laser printer, a laser disc player, a CD ROM drive and a laser pointer.

Many questioned the ultimate practicality of the laser and they kept comparing it to the transistor because the transistor went into practical applications quickly. By contrast, in their eyes, the laser was languishing.

I pointed out that laser applications are different. With transistors, there were some thirty years of electronics technology development with vacuum tubes prior to the advent of the transistor. A plethora of very sophisticated technology that was ready to use the transistor was already in place, such as telephones, radios and television. The early electronics design-engineer adopters could almost literally remove the vacuum tubes out of their sockets and replace them with transistors.

A better analogy for the laser might be the airplane. From the time of the Wright Brothers flight at Kitty Hawk in 1903 to the advent of commercial aviation was about 30 years. The airplane in its early days, was considered a toy, largely used for pleasure and excitement; acrobatic and stunt flying. For that matter, in the early days of the automobile, it was also not taken seriously; it was a play thing of the rich.

There was one place that lasers were analogous to transistors, that was in ophthalmology. A xenon arc lamp had been developed by Zeiss to repair detached retinas. It was obvious that the laser could not only do the same thing but that it would be a superior solution with much better control. This was possibly the first practical application of the laser, outside of its rapid adoption by research laboratories as a scientific investigative tool.

At first, lasers were used to accomplish specialized tasks, though not in high volume. A giant pulse laser with its ultra short pulse was used to balance a gyroscope on the fly, that is, while it was rotating at very high speeds. Defective welds in certain expensive vacuum tubes could be repaired without opening the tube, by focusing a laser beam through the envelope of the tube. Holes were drilled in diamonds to make diamond dies for drawing copper wire. Korad made and delivered several such diamond hole drillers. Korad also manufactured a laser welder since lasers can easily combine many material combinations that would otherwise be virtually impossible to weld.

The world's first lunar ranging system used a Korad very high-powered giant pulse laser to bounce light off a mirror planted on the moon by the astronaut crew of Apollo 11. The McDonald Astronomical Observatory at the University of Texas used that Korad laser for 20 years to obtain precise data regarding the distance and variations between the moon and the earth. Out at its 200,000 mile distance, measurements were made to a precision of a fraction of an inch. This historic system joined the Smithsonian Institution's collection of important scientific instruments when it was decommissioned and placed on exhibition by the Smithsonian Institution in 1985.

**The Laser Armada**

During the sixties, for the most part, laser uses were dominated by ruby lasers for power applications and the red version of the helium-neon laser for instrumentation. Many other lasers of different types were developed at a rapid pace. Most of these lasers turned out to be laboratory curiosities, but the noteworthy ones persisted and became the workhorses.

Elias Snitzer at the American Optical Company developed the first glass laser in 1961. Glass laser materials have very broad fluorescence levels. Consequently, they generally require large pump power by comparison to a similar crystal laser. Glass however, can be made to have almost perfect optical quality and it can also be manufactured into huge blanks not possible with crystal materials. The largest laser in the world is a glass laser at the Lawrence Livermore laboratory in California, it occupies the space of an entire building. The purpose of this laser is to do research with the hope of attaining so-called *laser fusion*. Laser fusion, if successful, would provide a clean and almost inexhaustible energy source.[85]

---

[85] As with the laser weapon, in my opinion, laser fusion is not a *practical* application for the laser.

Late in 1962, independently and almost simultaneously, four different laboratories produced the first semiconductor lasers. They were: Nick Holonyak at GE Syracuse; Marshall Nathan at IBM Yorktown Heights; Robert Hall at GE Schenectady; and T. M. Quist at MIT Lincoln Laboratories.

The early semiconductor lasers (also called diode lasers) were pulsed and cryogenically cooled. At first, they didn't appear to be especially practical. However, even the early semiconductor lasers exhibited comparatively high efficiencies of 25 to 50 percent, in contrast to the 1 to 5 percent efficiencies of crystal lasers. Over time, diode lasers matured. By 1975, they no longer needed to be pulsed or cooled. These diode lasers are now the most ubiquitous of all laser types. There are millions of these tiny lasers in CD/DVD players, laser printers, bar code readers and even laser pointers. The diode laser is also the driver for fiber-optic communications including telephones, televisions and data transmission. Higher power versions of these devices are now used widely in industry and medical surgery.

Lasers that use the energy levels of ions in gas discharges became useful because they were able to provide radiative power levels of many watts, as opposed to the milliwatts limitation provided from neutral atoms in gas discharges. The most important laser in this class is the argon ion laser developed in 1964 by Bill Bridges at Hughes Research Labs.

The deep infrared molecular carbon dioxide laser was developed in 1964 by Kumar Patel at Bell Telephone Laboratories. After refinement and maturation, this laser became very important in industry and surgery. Versions of the carbon dioxide laser are capable of multi-kilowatt (1000 watt) power levels.

The previously mentioned neodymium doped YAG laser also emerged from Bell Laboratories in 1964. The Nd-YAG laser is the practical embodiment of the "holy grail", the much sought after four-level crystal laser. It is free of cryogenics and operates with significantly less pump power than ruby. It is however, not without some limitations. High quality crystals of this material are difficult to grow and hence are rather costly. The radiation is in the infrared part of the spectrum where eyes, film and photoelectric cells are not very sensitive. However, this latter limitation was lifted when efficient non-linear materials were developed which magically, convert the infrared radiation to green light (as explained in the last chapter).

## Applications Begin

Widespread applications of laser started in the early 1970s. At that time, lasers became practical and reliable enough to be employed in industry on a regular basis. They were used to cut, weld, drill and mark a variety of materials.

An interesting application concept was its use to drill holes in turbine blades. Because of the curved shape of a turbine blade, a laser is a much more practical tool than a mechanical drill. Also, lasers, unlike drills, don't become dull with use.

Lasers were starting to be used in surgery as a nearly bloodless scalpel. The laser cauterizes as it cuts.

Robert Mauer and Donald Keck at Corning Glass developed the low-loss glass fiber in the early 1970s. This important breakthrough enabled the promise of the use of lasers in communications to proceed on the road to reality. It spawned the whole fiber-optics communications industry. Further, the Corning breakthrough allowed the use of glass fibers in surgical lasers to give the surgeon a flexible connection between the laser console and the laser scalpel.

During the 1970s and 1980s, the applications for lasers mushroomed into entertainment, science, communications, medicine, manufacturing, data processing, military usage and much more …

Today, the use of lasers is so pervasive in volume and breadth that we no longer have to defensively think of the laser as a "solution looking for a problem". On the contrary, a few years ago, I presented a paper at a conference titled Problems Found.

As I stated earlier, the laser is a rare example of a technology that not only has lived up to all the early hype, but has far exceeded that early hype beyond anyone's and certainly my expectations.

CHAPTER 22

# Hughes Patent Blunders

## Hughes Passes on Filing Patent

For new technical employees in most United States corporations, a condition of employment is the signing of an agreement that any patentable ideas of the employees become the property of the corporation. They must agree to assign the patent application and any and all potential rights to the corporation. This is done ahead of time just in case they create something. Since the employee is not in a negotiating position at the onset of employment, it is a questionable practice. As a matter of principle, I was reluctant to sign the contract agreement when I joined Hughes and, as I remember, I refused to do so.

As part of corporate procedure, when employees submit papers for journal publication, the papers must be routed through the corporate patent department for approval. Then the patent department, with the help of management, makes a determination as to whether the work is new and novel and if, it has importance to the corporation. If it passes that test, patent applications are prepared with the help of the employees and submitted to the United States Patent Office. Only then are the papers cleared for publication.

Importance to the corporation could be direct use of the invention in its own business. Even if there is not a direct use connection, a fundamental patent could be useful to a corporation as a lucrative source of licensing royalty income. The more significant patents are also submitted for foreign patent coverage.

In my case, when I submitted my paper describing the first laser for publication, the patent department signed off, giving permission to publish. *Hughes chose not to file any applications at that time.*

There are consequences. Most foreign patent rights are lost as soon as publication or public disclosure occurs, unless the patent is already on file. With regard to the United States Patent Office, one year is permitted after public disclosure.

When I announced to Hughes in April of 1961 that I was leaving the company, they immediately decided, at this late date to write a patent disclosure and file for my patent. They had already forfeited the possibility of foreign patents and the clock was running on United States patents.

## A Question of Ownership

Dan Anderson, a patent attorney at Hughes Aircraft, brought me my patent disclosure. He wanted me to edit the disclosure and sign the application for submission to the United States Patent Office. He also brought the papers for my assignment and transfer of all patent rights to Hughes. I told him that I wasn't willing to sign over the rights to Hughes "You have to!" He said. "You signed an agreement to that effect when you joined Hughes."

"I don't think I did," I replied.

The next day Dan returned to my office, white as a sheet. *"You're right, we couldn't find it!* But, it doesn't matter, you have to assign it to Hughes anyway. When you work for a company and create patentable ideas, they belong to the company." He continued: "If you don't sign, we will come after you, we will win, you will just get a bad reputation." He was persuasive, I signed.

About six years later, I received a letter from Dan Anderson. He said that he had also left Hughes and was in private law practice. He explained that when he had advised me to assign the laser patent to Hughes he fully believed what he had told me, that is, that I had no other options. But recently, he had found that he had not been correct. If I had not signed the pre-agreement I was not obligated to assign the patent to Hughes. Dan said that he was willing to sign an affidavit testifying to the fact that he had wrongfully advised me, had, in fact, coerced me to sign and also that he had not advised me to get my own counsel. Dan did prepare and sign such an affidavit.

When I received this information, I was president of Korad Inc. I took the information to Ralph Pastorisa, the Korad patent attorney and asked for advice. Ralph agreed with Anderson's analysis and suggested that I proceed against Hughes. I concurred and Ralph notified Hughes of the new status.

Ralph also wrote the United States Patent Office on my behalf and asked that he be appointed co-counsel with Hughes on the patent application. He requested, however, that all ongoing communication regarding the patent be sent to Hughes.

Hughes responded that they knew about the mix up that occurred when I resigned, but that they had since found the pre-employment assignment agreement and sent over the purported document. Ralph attempted to check out the witness on the document and could not find any such person. Hughes then asserted that we didn't read the signature correctly and it was another person, whom they produced.

Ralph then hired a forgery expert to determine if my signature was authentic. Based on the photocopy sent to us, the expert decided that as far as he could ascertain it was my signature. Of course, Hughes had many copies of my signature in their files.

## Saving the Patent for Hughes

In the meantime, the U.S. Patent Office misunderstood Ralph's letter and sent the next office action to us at Korad instead as instructed to Hughes. The Patent Office action stated that my application was obvious and quoted references to Wieder and Schawlow-Townes. This is standard Patent Office position language, it is their job to be in effect, the devil's advocate. Nonetheless, I saw red—if it was so obvious, why didn't *they* do it?

Apparently, Hughes had been jousting with the Patent Office over a six year period and had not been persuasive enough to get the patent issued.

I immediately prepared a reply in which each of the Patent Office's objections was addressed and answered, each and every one of them in detail.

I showed my response to Ralph. He was extremely impressed and said that with essentially no change, he would make my statements into an affidavit. "Your answers to the office action are very persuasive. If we submit your response, in all likelihood your patent will be issued," he said.

But, he said, now you have a decision to make; it doesn't look like we will prevail in a patent ownership action against Hughes. If that's the case, do you still want to submit the affidavit? Of course, your name will still be on the patent, even if it is assigned to Hughes. They can't change that, but, you will get nothing out of it. What do you want to do?

I stewed over that decision for a day or two and decided to go ahead.

Ralph wrote to Hughes, explaining how we had incorrectly received the Patent Office's final rejection notice and offered the affidavit to Hughes for response to the Patent Office. Ralph further advised Hughes, if they refused, we would send the affidavit directly—he could do this, since he was now my co-attorney.

Hughes was ecstatic. They accepted our offer and filed my affidavit. Within five weeks, the patent was issued.[86]

## National Inventors Hall of Fame

About ten years later, when I was Vice-President for Advanced Technology at TRW, I became acquainted with one of the their patent attorneys, Larry Cohen.

Larry decided that he wanted to submit my name in nomination, based on my laser patent, to the National Inventors Hall of Fame. This is a very big honor. Of the more than 5 million United States Patents issued at that time, only about 50 inventors had been inducted into the National Inventors Hall of Fame. Well known inductees included Thomas Alva Edison, Alexander Graham Bell and the Wright Brothers.

Larry successfully submitted the application. The President of the National Inventors Hall of Fame notified me that there would be a black tie dinner and an important ceremony for my induction in Washington, D.C.

The National Inventors Hall of Fame Foundation is poorly financed, so they ask the companies who own the relevant patent to pay the bill for transportation and for the table at the dinner. The inventor is given a quota of people who can be invited to the dinner. I invited my daughter and son-in-law and of course, Larry Cohen.

---

[86] Hughes paid me a total of three hundred dollars for my patent.

Hughes executives had a fit. TRW is a Hughes competitor and Hughes didn't want to pay for Larry's transportation; even though by now both Larry and I had left TRW.

## Hughes' Embarrassment

I had a conversation with one of the Hughes patent attorneys before the induction ceremony. He said that Hughes was embarrassed. I wondered to myself but not aloud, why?

Was it because Hughes had forfeited the foreign patents?

Was it due to the fact Hughes didn't file the patent application until I announced that I was leaving the company and then just got under the one year time limit wire for the United States filing?

Was it that Hughes had so ineptly prosecuted the patent with the Patent Office that it was in danger of final rejection and that only through a quirk of circumstance did I save the patent for them?

The Hughes attorney stated, "They were embarrassed because Hughes had not had the foresight to nominate you for the National Inventors Hall of Fame."

Union Carbide later offered to buy my laser patent from Hughes. Hughes refused and said that, at the time, it was the most lucrative patent in their possession.

## Kathleen

The ceremony weekend turned out to be an especially pleasurable and momentous one for me.

During our time in Washington, my daughter, son-in-law and I visited the Smithsonian Space Museum. I was especially fascinated with the inner workings of a helicopter that was shown in great cutaway detail. I was taken with the idea of devising a simplified structure that might be quieter and more reliable than the standard helicopter design.

On the flight back from Washington's Dulles Airport to Los Angeles, I started to make some calculations based on ideas I was incubating about vertical takeoff aircraft. Aerodynamics is distant from my field of expertise, but I enjoy an interesting challenge.

Although a movie was playing on the screen in the front of the Boeing 747 aircraft, I didn't have my earphones on. From time to time, though, I would glance at the screen to see what seemed like an interesting plot.

I had recently halfway read through a book titled, *Drawing on the Right Side of Your Brain* by Betty Edwards. There was a particular statue shown over and over again in the movie and I tried to make a drawing of the statue. (Drawing is not my talent.)

I was sitting on the port side of the aircraft. I had already spotted a very attractive redhead on the opposite, or starboard side.

So ... my attention was divided three ways: I was watching the gorgeous young woman, calculating a new aircraft design and "drawing on the right side of my brain."

As the flight continued, I became more and more enthralled with the young woman. I tried to get her attention, but to no avail. I took a "stroll" on the other side of the aircraft and again I didn't get her attention (she was reading a book). I couldn't think of a good introductory line and I was reluctant to interrupt her.

Finally, as we landed and she gathered her things together in preparation for exit from the aircraft, I did get her attention. I smiled at her and got a spine tingling smile in return. With that encouragement, I made sure that we would walk together toward the baggage claim. As we proceeded and started to converse, I was even more taken with her. I became tongue-tied, she led the conversation.

She asked, "Were you in Washington to complete a million-dollar deal?"

"No."

"Were you here because your daughter just had a baby?"

"No."

"Were you in town to have dinner with the President?"

"You're getting closer." President Reagan had planned to attend the award ceremony and formal dinner but didn't show up.

As soon as I heard her first words, I thought to myself, "Wow, I'm in love."

As I got to know Kathleen, her creativity, her active enquiring mind, her sense of humor and her admirable sense of values, she became more and more irresistible.

When we were married in a private ceremony in Las Vegas, Nevada, the normally bored, commissioner of marriage took a steadied look at Kathleen and then back over to me. He broke into a smile and exclaimed, "Good move Theodore!"

Kathleen and I have been seldom separated since our fateful meeting on February 13, 1984.

CHAPTER 23

# The Paper Patents

I have never encountered any controversy as to the fact that I created the world's first laser. It's also a fact that I obtained a patent on that laser and it was assigned to Hughes Aircraft Company. As a result of that issued and validated patent, I was installed in the National Inventors Hall of Fame.

Does that mean that I am the *inventor* of the laser?

There have been various other laser patents issued and I have often been asked about the status of these other patents, on how they fit into the complex and controversial patent picture?

In this chapter, that part of the laser story as I know it will be explained. After you read it, you can decide the answers to the questions posed above.

## Patent Categories

When inventors file an application for patent protection for their new concepts with the United States Patent Office, several conditions must be met in order to determine whether patents are issued.

First and foremost, the concept must be new. In addition, the device must either have been reduced to practice (a prototype made that clearly demonstrates the principle or the idea); or, if the device has not been reduced to practice, the patent disclosure must provide *teachings*.

For this purpose, teachings are defined as information provided in the patent application, sufficient for a person skilled in the art, to glean enough knowledge from the patent application, that they can reduce it to practice without the need for additional invention. A person skilled in the art, is someone knowledgeable in the field covered by the patent. An issued patent that has not been reduced to practice, but rather is based solely on teachings, is referred to as a *paper patent*.

The patent examiner takes an adversarial or "devil's advocate" position in order to effectively screen out inventions that already exist. Patent examiners do the best they can, but the budget and resources of the United States Patent Office are limited. It's not one of the *in* departments when it comes to government spending (like the space program, for example).

Many dubious patent disclosures get through the Patent Office and become issued patents. But when these patents are tested, they do not survive. A patent may be tested when the patent owner asserts rights against a potential patent infringer. That is, a user of the patent who refuses to pay royalties, starting a legal battle that may be settled only by a court ruling. In that situation, the judge determines whether or not the user is infringing on the patent as it exists, or that the patent, even though issued, is not valid.

The non-validity of a patent can be argued on a number of grounds, such as prior patents that were not caught by the patent examiner, or that the patent information already existed in the public domain prior to the issuance of the patent, or that the patent needed additional invention. A successful argument in either case results in an invalid patent. Some 80 percent of patents that are tested and challenged in court are thrown out.

The most contentious can often be the patents that are issued on the basis of teachings, that is, patents *not* reduced to practice, the paper patents. These paper patents are more vulnerable to challenge because if the patentees really knew how to make the alleged new device, then in all likelihood they would have reduced it to practice.

### The Schawlow-Townes Patent

In July 1959, Schawlow and Townes submitted a patent disclosure to the United States Patent Office based on their paper in *Physical Review* that is discussed in Chapter 19. They claimed the potassium-pumped-potassium system and it was indeed issued to them and assigned to Bell Telephone Laboratories in March 1960. However, this patent disclosure does not describe a workable system. Not only was their patent not reduced to practice at the time the patent disclosure was filed; *it was never reduced to practice.*

This was the first laser patent actually issued. Bell Labs and Schawlow-Townes use this fact and allege that they are the co-inventors of the laser. But are they? Of course not.

*Where is the laser that Schawlow and Townes invented?*

This is great spin but misleading to the scientific community and to the general public.

As it turns out, the patent was never tested. By that I mean that no supposed patent infringer was approached by Bell Labs and asked to pay royalties. Why is that? Bell Labs has never been known to be shy about collecting royalties on their patents. They obviously did not want their paper patent tested. If the patent were tested in court and it failed and was thrown out, then Bell would lose the public relations value of being able to say that this is the first laser patent.

*My investigative research indicates that no company or individual has ever paid royalties on the Schawlow-Townes patent.*

Thus, the Schawlow-Townes, Bell Labs patent was not valuable from the standpoint of the usual criteria for patents, the ability to produce a royalty stream. But, the patent has been of inestimable value as a public relations ploy, even though, it does not work.

## Gordon Gould Patent

The Gould Patent should in reality, be in the same boat as the Schawlow-Townes patent, but the story is more complicated and has an amazing ending.

In 1957, Gordon Gould, a graduate student at Columbia University, came up with proposed suggestions regarding creation of a laser. The underlying basis of the Gould concept was strikingly similar to Schawlow-Townes proposals. As a result, over the years Gould and Schawlow-Townes have been at each other's throats, each claiming to have hatched the idea.

The highlight of the Gould patent disclosure was an alkali vapor system proposal similar to the Schawlow-Townes proposal. The difference was that, Gould proposed using a sodium discharge lamp to pump a sodium vapor-cell instead of the potassium-pumped-potassium scheme of Schawlow-Townes.

The sodium system, like the potassium system, also was never reduced to practice. Gould, with due respect, did have far more in his patent disclosure than did Schawlow-Townes. Nevertheless, none of the systems described by Gould provided sufficient teachings to make a laser.

What I mean by that is, although Gould went beyond the alkali-alkali schemes to a number of gas discharge ideas, in no case were there given the important parameters of gas pressures, discharge currents, pressure ratios, etc. Moreover, he didn't provide calculations for the gain coefficients which are of critical importance to a specific laser design. They are the go, or no go, determinants for a workable model.

In short, no one skilled in the art, including Gould, could deduce from the Gould patent disclosure which, if any, of the "laundry list" of systems he proposed could really work. There were insufficient specifics on how to indeed make a laser. Therefore, no patent should have been issued.

Gould filed repeatedly with the Patent Office in attempts to get one or more patents for his ideas. As should have been expected, he was regularly turned down. No real surprise here.

When he appealed the adverse decisions, the appellate court also ruled against him. The appellate court noted that Gould's company, TRG, with some 35 technologists, had worked diligently on his proposed schemes and in the process consumed contract funds of $1 million (1959) dollars. Nonetheless, TRG did not succeed in making a laser.

Gould retorted that he was not able to work on the patent ideas himself because of a security clearance problem (the TRG contract was classified). There are five points that argue against this position.

Point one: Gould *did* work in a separate unclassified laboratory at TRG.

Point two: Although Gould could not ask questions of the classified researchers, they *could* ask questions of him.

Point three: The TRG scientists not only had access to Gould's patent disclosure but, in addition, they had total access to Gould's notes and other information not included in the patent application.

Point four: The requirement of *teachings* in a paper patent disclosure requires that *people skilled in the art are able to make the alleged invention strictly from the information disclosed in the patent application*. That means without the benefit of private notebooks, development of new technology, or further invention.

Point five: Even with all the help well beyond the patent disclosure and more than adequate funding, as noted by the appellate court, Gould's colleagues at TRG still failed to make a laser.

TRG was acquired by Control Data Corporation who became the owner of all rights to the Gould patent applications. Thereafter, Control Data fought a number of expensive legal battles on behalf of the Gould patent disclosures but to no avail. They finally gave up.

At that time, Gould offered to buy back the rights to his disclosures for some token amount. Control Data agreed to his terms.

Gould then found another patent attorney, Richard Samuel. In return for a major interest in any patent rights, Samuel agreed to take over. Samuel came up with a very clever idea, a concept that turned out to be an inconceivably brilliant masterstroke. He argued: Since the Patent Office is adamant about not issuing a patent for a laser based on Gould's applications, let's reapply once more to the Patent Office, but not ask for coverage for a laser. *Instead, we will ask only for rights to a light amplifier.*

It worked!

A patent examiner, much to his later regret and consternation, threw Gould a bone. He (the examiner) allowed the *amplifier* patent to issue.

Samuel then declared, "Aha! We have them!" Since all lasers have an amplifier within, we can assert our light amplifier patent claims against all users of lasers.

The Patent Office regretted its mistake and, the laser community went into shock, totally in disagreement with the patent examiner's decision. The commissioner of patents also disagreed with the turn of events.

## A Travesty of Justice

When it realized what it had done, the Patent Office nullified the patent. But, by now Samuel had raised considerable capital through a public stock offering based solely on Gould's amplifier patent. The majority owner of Gould's patent rights, the REFAC Technology Development Corporation of New York, now had more legal financial resources than the United States Patent Office! (which as already indicated is a poorly financed government agency.)

The Patent Office mustered only a weak defense in the REFAC appeal. The United States Patent Office lost.

Now it was time to test the patent in court. REFAC asserted its Gould patent rights and demanded a sizable royalty payment against a small laser company, called Control Laser located in Orlando, Florida. Control Laser refused to give royalty payments. REFAC demanded a jury trial.

Control Laser hired me as an expert witness to testify on their behalf. During the pretrial discovery period, I was deposed in Orlando. By going through the experience of the deposition in Florida, I was afforded the opportunity to discern the litigation skills of the REFAC attorney as well as these of the Control Laser attorney, Bob Duckworth.

I was extremely impressed with the REFAC attorney, but not so with Duckworth. He sat through my whole question and answer period without saying a word. After the deposition, he complained to me that I had answered a trick question without realizing the import of my answer. Why didn't he speak up *during* the deposition and request a clarification of the question?

I complained to Robbie Van Roijen, the Chairman of Control Laser, but he was satisfied with and committed to Duckworth.

I started to think a bit about the overall picture. What was bothering me were the following issues:

On the witness stand at trial I would be fully prepared to present technical testimony and to respond to challenges to that testimony. But I didn't expect to be subjected to personal attacks, which I found to be the case during the deposition. Bob Duckworth just sat there without any objection.

I was concerned about the competence of the Control Laser legal team. I wasn't excited about going through the aggravation of a courtroom trial with low probability of success.

Duckworth had stated to me that, in his opinion, I was the only one in the whole world who could convincingly knock out the Gould patent. He explained: who could possibly be better to challenge the concept of whether there were *adequate teachings* in the Gould patent disclosure than the person who actually made the first laser?

I decided to bow out of testifying in court. I declined to testify.

This was a poor decision!

Charles Townes was hired as Control Laser's expert witness in my stead. Peter Franken was the expert witness for REFAC. *As far as I know, neither Franken nor Townes had ever made a laser.*

I knew Peter Franken from when I was a graduate student at Stanford. He was a new addition to the Stanford Physics Department faculty, recently arrived from Columbia University, where he had studied for his doctorate.

Peter was extremely personable, interesting, engaging, provocative and sometimes downright outrageous. It's unlikely that anyone could be around Peter for more than a few minutes without laughing. He had a great sense of humor and a dry wit.

Peter Franken was a very fine scientist. He earned a strong reputation as Deputy Director of ARPA; president of the American Optical Society; and director of the Optical Sciences Center at the University of Arizona. It was Peter Franken who, in effect, initiated the field of non-linear optics. As noted earlier, it was he who first produced optical harmonics when he generated ultraviolet light by passing the output of a high-power ruby laser through a quartz crystal.

Yet, in the pre-laser days of speculation about the possibility of generating coherent light (1959-1960), Peter Franken was one of its prominent doubters. As I mentioned earlier, he had a lecture scheduled for presentation at the University of Michigan, where he was a professor of physics at the time, in late summer of 1960. The lecture was an argument *against* the likelihood of a laser ever becoming a reality.

My July 1960 laser announcement preceded his intended lecture. *He was saved by the bell.*

Expert witness was also a peculiar position for Charles Townes. If Townes could make a convincing argument that Gould did not have sufficient teachings in his patent disclosure, then his same reasoning would apply to the Schawlow-Townes patent, only in spades!

There is no question in my mind. Neither patent had the teachings required to qualify as valid. Nevertheless, REFAC won the case.

Some years later, Robbie Van Roijen told me that the Control Laser Board caved in and settled before the jury decided on the penalty phase of the trial. He said that afterwards the jury foreman asked why Control Laser didn't wait for the penalty decision. *The jury had planned to award one dollar to REFAC!*

REFAC, Samuel and Gould, collectively took in about $100 million in royalties over the 17-year patent life. Patlex, a company that combined the interests of Gould, Samuel and REFAC, owns and collects the patent royalties.

Gould actually benefited from the long delay in the issuance of his patent. Due to a quirk in prior patent law, the 17-year license period for a patent started when the patent was issued. When Gould's patent finally became effective, the laser industry was quite mature. As a result, the royalty flow was considerably higher than it would have been had the patent been issued in the usual one to three years.

Patent law has since changed: The time of validity for a patent is now 20 years, but the clock starts at the time of application. Had the new law been in force, Gould would have collected little or nothing because the clock would have run out.

Gordon Gould has three people to thank for his success in the patent litigation matter.

First, Dick Samuel, not only for his brilliant idea, which confused the Patent Office with the idea of the light amplifier, but also, his successful idea to raise a considerable war chest of funds for the legal battle.

Second, Peter Franken, for his expert witness testimony. I'm not sure that REFAC could have found another scientist with such substantial credentials who would have agreed to do that.

Third, me, for my decision *not* to testify.

In hindsight, I am convinced that I could have been persuasive at the trial and prevailed, despite the shortcomings of the Control Laser legal team. The decision that I made was a poor one. At this point however, it is water over the bridge, since the patent has now expired.

In my view, the Gould patent affair was a travesty of justice.

CHAPTER 24

# Award Happenings

I have been fortunate enough to be honored with a number of awards and scientific prizes that recognize my development of the first laser.

In this chapter, I tell about the highlights of three of those awards, because of their particular significance and interesting details.

### The Hertz & LBJ

John Hertz founded the yellow taxicab company, where he made his fortune. Later, he founded Hertz Rent-a-Car and multiplied his assets further.

John and his wife Fanny set up a foundation to further and encourage science students. In 1965 the Hertz Foundation initiated the Fannie & John Hertz Science Award.

I was notified that I was a recipient of the award for my work in developing the first laser and was told that the award would be given at a White House ceremony. It was to be bestowed by President Lyndon B. Johnson. The award ceremonies would continue on the following day with an elaborate black-tie dinner and formal award ceremony.

Then I learned that I was to share the prize and cash award of $20,000 with another scientist, Ali Javan. I was puzzled and angry. I had already become inured to occasional credit controversies with Schawlow and Townes. But Javan? Some politics had to be in play here.

Javan did not make the first laser. And Javan did not make the second or third laser. He made the *fourth* laser, which was the first to use gas as the laser medium. Apparently, not taken into account, was the fact that my achievement and subsequent announcement of the first laser, sparked the later development of those other lasers.

There was obviously something awry here. I thought of declining the invitation, but it was hard to bypass an award distinguished by the symbolism and recognition of the President of the United States.

More details emerged; I was told I would be cited second at the awards ceremony because they explained it would be alphabetical order (when chronological would have made more sense.)

It got worse; a press release was published in The *New York Times*. In the *Times* story, Javan was heralded as receiving the Hertz Award in a White House ceremony for his laser development. At the bottom of the story, the last line stated, "Maiman will also be getting an award."

I have to admit I went out of control. To make an award to Javan for the first laser was already appalling, but this latest development was more than I was willing to put up with. I called the Hertz committee and told them they could keep the medal and the $10,000 cash prize. I declined to appear at the award banquet. I said I would return to California and hold my own press conference.

The committee members were shocked and requested that I meet with them for a debriefing, which I did. I don't remember all of the names of the people in attendance, but I do remember Edward Teller, *father of the H-bomb*. Professor Teller was one of the Hertz foundation trustees.

There were several other board members there as well. One of these members took the lead in questioning me; he was clearly an attorney. I presented the facts of my complaint and said I assumed that Charles Townes, one of the foundation trustees somehow was involved.

Edward Teller remarked, "Well, Charlie does have an ax to grind."

The attorney declared: "You are impugning the integrity of a Nobel Laureate."

"He's human, isn't he?" I rejoined.

"You are questioning the integrity of the entire award committee, not just Townes. The full committee voted this way," said the attorney.

"Wait a second," I said. "I have a hunch it went something like this: The committee first agreed that the award should be for the first laser and then probably turned to Townes to decide on who should receive the award."

My statement astonished the attorney.

"Yes, that was exactly what happened!" he then confided. "Townes came forward with three possible recommendations: 1) Maiman alone; 2) Maiman and Javan or 3) Maiman, Javan, Bennett and Herriott.

As expected, they took the middle ground.

I explained that I alone had made the first laser in May 1960 and that Javan's laser was the *fourth* laser. I explained that Bell Labs had been on the verge of canceling the funding for the Javan project, which was languishing when my news release appeared.

Since it is so telling a description of the mood at Bell Labs and the unreality of the gas laser development at that time, I repeat again the quote made by, Bill Bennett, one of Javan's collaborators on the principal gas laser effort at Bell Labs in an interview with *Science* magazine.

"An atmosphere of skepticism about laser oscillators pervaded Bell Laboratories before Maiman's announcement. At one point, the Bell administration considered cutting off funds for research on the helium neon laser, just months before it was made to work. It was only after Maiman demonstrated that a laser actually could be built that the clouds of skepticism lifted. Then money quickly became available for all kinds of laser projects."

After the news release of my ruby laser, the gas laser team at Bell now knew for sure that a laser could be made. Bell Labs shifted gears and pushed Javan's development hard. Javan, Bennett and Herriott were subsequently successful in making a gas laser in the end of December 1960: seven and a half months after I put my ruby laser into operation.

I asked, "Did Townes point out that he had an apparent 'conflict of interest' and disclose that Javan and Bennett were essentially part of his 'academic family?' They had been his graduate students at

Columbia. Also, that he (Townes) was now in effect, Javan's boss since Townes was at this time Provost and, Javan was a professor at MIT.

Townes had not disclosed this information to the committee.

The committee investigated my accusations and became angry with Townes. They called him in Boston and expressed their disappointment.

As a result, the citation presentation order was reversed. My citation was given first and the content was changed to be heavily in my favor. Of course, damage had already been done because the press release was not corrected.

At the award ceremony, I sat at the dais on stage next to Edward Teller. He said that he was able to empathize with me because, during his own career, he had had a similar experience.

*Once again, I found what it was like to butt against the establishment*

## The Wolf Prize

It is a great honor to receive the Wolf Prize. The late Ricardo Wolf, a wealthy, self-made industrialist, diplomat and philanthropist, established the Wolf Foundation in 1967. This Israel-based private foundation mandated the issuance of annual awards to individuals who made important contributions to the fields of chemistry, medicine, mathematics, physics, arts and agriculture in 1978. The nominees and their work are scrutinized so that the awards all carry equal prestige to the Nobel Prize given in Sweden.

I was delighted to hear that I was chosen to receive a Wolf Prize in physics in 1984. An interesting coincidence and pleasant surprise was the discovery that the Wolf Foundation was also honoring my friend Irwin Hahn at the same time. Irwin was now a professor of physics at the University of California, Berkeley. He was recognized for his very basic *spin-echo* work, fundamental to MRI (Magnetic Resonance Imaging), the medical diagnostic tool.

I very much looked forward to seeing Irwin again. I was still indebted to him for his recommendation and his referral of me to the Hughes Research Laboratory's Atomic Physics Department. And I was especially eager to see Irwin since I remembered our camaraderie at Stanford and Irwin's outrageously engaging personality.

We were, indeed able to renew our friendship, reminisce and recall the jokes of the Stanford days.

## The Japan Prize

In 1984 the Science and Technology Foundation of Japan initiated a series of prizes to be awarded, modeled to the stature and prestige level of the famous Swedish Nobel Prize.

The Japan Prize is awarded annually; it was established and funded by the self-made billionaire Mr. Matsushita, chairman and founder of the Matsushita Corporation, the largest electronics company in Japan. Matsushita is the parent company of the Panasonic and Technic electronics product lines.

Mr. Matsushita declined to have the prize in his name as did Nobel in Sweden. Instead, in modesty, he favored calling it the *Japan Prize*. The Japanese often refer to their prize as the "Nobel of the East."

Although the Japan Prize is not as well known to the public as the Nobel, it carries the same status in the scientific community. The Nobel Laureates go to Sweden and receive their award from the King of Sweden. The Emperor of Japan honors the Japan Prize Laureates.

I was a designated laureate of the Japan Prize in 1987; Dr. Michael Barnoski had successfully nominated me. Mike is an internationally acclaimed author and expert in the field of fiber-optics. We had worked together at the international conglomerate TRW and also at a fiber-optic venture, PCO, that Mike had founded. He, I and our wives Barbara and Kathleen, are all close friends.

I was chosen to receive the Japan Prize in the field of electro-optics and was invited to Tokyo where the prize was to be awarded. My wife Kathleen and I and my daughter Sheri and son-in-law Jeff, traveled together to attend the weeklong celebration in Japan.

The Japan Prize was a singular honor, our trip had several highlights.

## Emperor Hirohito

One of those highlights was a private audience at the royal palace with His Majesty, Emperor Hirohito of Japan.

Kathleen and I stood in a reception room with two other laureates and their wives. The two others were sharing a Japan Prize in another category.

The Emperor approached us with an interpreter at his side. He very politely asked each of us in turn questions about our work. The Emperor, himself a marine biologist, could ask questions as one scientist to another. Emperor Hirohito had been personally responsible for the identification of more than 40 new marine species.

As the Emperor proceeded along the line there was not much expression on his face. But, as he came along side of me, he looked past me to Kathleen. His eyes widened and a clear smile came over his face, as he viewed the gorgeous brown-eyed redhead draped in her beautiful turquoise gown.

I was awestruck by my thoughts. I was standing face to face with a man who, on the one hand, was only a figurehead at this point but nevertheless was still a deity to the Japanese people. Emperor Hirohito had been the ruler of Japan when Pearl Harbor was attacked in 1941, throughout and after World War II.

As I watched him staring at my wife, I was engrossed in my thoughts and buffered by emotion. Questions were racing through my mind. What was the Emperor's role in the attack of December 7, 1941? Was that strictly a military operation of the Imperial War Lords, one that he had no control of and maybe did not even know about until afterward? Or, was he more deeply involved? I couldn't help but think about this entire subject, as I observed in front of me a gentle scientist, only one year older than my own father, also a scientist.

### The Red Tie Affair

Our entourage, which consisted of the Japan Prize Laureates and our families, had been in the custody of the administrative secretary for the Science and Technology Foundation of Japan.

The laureates were asked to present several speeches at the ceremony and to participate in a number of academic seminars. The administrator ran an extremely close-watched, rigorous schedule. After one speech, he complained not jokingly that I had spoken for only 27 minutes and that the allotted time had been 30 minutes. It was a concrete example of Japanese exactitude.

The award ceremony was an elaborate, formal, black-tie occasion. When we approached the time for the ceremony, I explained to the foundation administrator that although I would comply with the wearing of a tuxedo for this formal affair, I planned to wear a red bow-tie and handkerchief. Was that acceptable? The administrator went into shock! "You don't have a *black* bow-tie?" He sputtered.

"No." I replied." Actually, I did have a black bow-tie in my pocket. I was testing.

He was adamant: "You must have a black bow-tie, I will purchase one for you."

"No, I think it will be okay, I will be formally attired," I explained, "and besides, I asked the personal secretary of the Foundation President, she said it would be okay."

"She doesn't have any authority in this matter!" cried the Administrator.

"I think it will be okay," I said.

When we entered into the auditorium, the members of the selection and award committee were seated on stage at the back. They *all* wore black bow-ties. Only high-level dignitaries were invited to the award ceremony and all the men in the audience also wore *black* bow-ties.

On the stage were: His Highness, the Crown Prince Akihito and Her Highness, the Crown Princess Michiko; Mr. Matsushita, President of the Science and Technology Foundation; and the three laureates and their spouses.

Now, finally, I began to feel uncomfortable. I was the only man in the auditorium who was not wearing a black bow-tie!

Mr. Matsushita was seated in a wheelchair. When it came time to present my citation, he arose and came forward. I had memorized an appropriate thank you in Japanese and recited it when Mr. Matsushita handed me my award. He didn't seem impressed with my Japanese since he had a very passive look on his face.

Suddenly, he spotted my red handkerchief and red bow-tie. A big smile came over his face and he reached over and touched the red handkerchief. We left the stage in an orderly recession and, I was directed to follow behind Her Highness, Princess Michiko. Mr. Matsushita was in his wheelchair at the head of the receiving line and was acknowledging the members of the procession. As we walked past, the Crown Princess stepped forward to pay her respects to Mr. Matsushita. She turned back to me and said, "He likes your red bow-tie and handkerchief!"

I was vindicated!

Later that same evening, the foundation administrator spoke with me and asked: "Dr. Maiman, is it true that you wear the red bow-tie to signify the red ruby laser?"

I said "yes!"

The incident did not go unnoticed. The next day at a press conference, the Japanese reporters wanted to know what Mr. Matsushita had said to me when he touched my red handkerchief at the award ceremony. Of course I didn't know, since he spoke in Japanese.

There was a large and lavish banquet dinner held after the award ceremony, with probably 1000 people in attendance. I was seated between the Japanese Chief Justice on my left and on my right was Her Highness Michiko, the Crown Princess (and now Empress) of Japan. The conversation with Her Highness was very stimulating and I found her to be a fascinating and charming woman.

Opposite of me at the center of the long table was His Highness Akihito, the Crown Prince, now The Emperor of Japan and also a marine biologist. He sat next to and conversed mostly with Kathleen about the marine species in and around Japan. He also spoke proudly of Her Highness, Princess Michiko, and her talents with the cello.

My daughter and son-in-law were not seated at our table, but with another interesting group in this very large room.

Sheri and Jeff rejoined Kathleen and me after the banquet. We had all planned to go together to the post-banquet cocktail party. On their arrival they were barred from joining us by security guards. Her Highness, the Crown Princess, intervened, "Let the children in!" She saw to it that Sheri and Jeff could stay with us at the cocktail party, an act of kindness that was very much appreciated.

The entire trip to Japan was most memorable.

## Tragedy Strikes

Looking back, one of the very pleasing aspects of the trip to Japan was the fact that my daughter Sheri was able to be on that trip with us. She delighted in visiting Japan and was so proud of me for getting the Japan Prize.

We received terrible news in the latter part of that same year. Sheri was diagnosed with terminal cancer. She fought very hard and bravely until her so untimely death less than one year later. I can't say that I have ever been able to truly recover from that tragic blow.

CHAPTER 25

# South America Adventure

## Backdrop

Over a period of several years, I was a participant in two medical laser societies. One of these, the YAG Laser Society, founded by laser surgeon Stephen N. Joffe, concentrates its attention on the use of YAG lasers in medicine. I was, in fact, introduced to laser medicine when Steve Joffe invited me to be the featured dinner speaker at the YAG Society's inaugural meeting.

The other society, the International Society for Laser Medicine and Surgery, founded by laser surgeon Isaac Kaplan, has a broader outlook on the different lasers used in medicine, Doctor Kaplan is generally recognized as the "father" of laser surgery.

These societies would often invite me to give one of the featured talks at the start of their meetings. As a result, my wife Kathleen and I were afforded the opportunity to travel to a number of interesting places around the globe, including Japan, Taiwan, Thailand, Germany and a number of different United States locations.

In November 1989, I was invited to present the opening lecture at the Eighth Congress of the International Society for Laser Medicine and Surgery held in Taipei, Taiwan. On our trip to Taipei, we flew aboard a commercial Boeing 747. As the aircraft was coming in for a landing, it lifted back off the ground at touchdown and then landed at a different part of the airport. I told Kathleen that the pilot seemed to be practicing "touch and go." We soon discovered that our plane had been diverted to a VIP gate. I wondered what celebrity must be on board when I spotted a television camera crew.

When Kathleen and I exited out of the airplane, the TV crew approached us and I realized that Taipei Television was covering our trip. We were interviewed as we walked into the terminal and we were led past customs and immigration very quickly. Normally, this is a very long procedure in Taipei.

We were led to a limousine and with the help of a police escort and the liberal use of their sirens, we quickly navigated rush-hour traffic. Taiwan President Lee Teng-hui had generously provided the limousine for us.

The next day, when we took in the daily newspaper outside of our hotel room door, we were startled to see our picture displayed prominently on the front page.

When we attended the various international meetings, we were often treated to beautifully presented talent shows characteristic of the country. It seemed as though all of the meeting organizers competed in showmanship to see if they could creatively outdo each other. We were the beneficiaries of that competition. It was truly impressive.

## Paraguay

Early in 1993 I received a call from Hugo Juri, President of the South American Division of the International Laser Society. He was planning to add a new section to the society for laser medicine, in Paraguay. Hugo asked me if I would come to Paraguay and present the opening paper for the first meeting of the new society. He mentioned that there would also be a brief trip to Argentina for some sightseeing.

I was a bit concerned and somewhat hesitant, since Paraguay was a military state ruled by a dictator. Kathleen and I discussed the possible trip and decided in favor of an anticipated adventure. I agreed to Hugo's request to give the opening lecture.

On arrival in Paraguay I learned that I was scheduled not only for the introductory talk, but in addition, I was on the schedule for two more papers that I hadn't prepared for. In fact, it appeared that I was on for the entire program the morning of the first day of the conference.

I was a bit miffed. This was more than I had agreed to and I wasn't prepared for the two extra lectures. But I was committed and did the best that I could and, with an optimistic outlook everything turned out fine that morning.

That Paraguay was a military state was apparent when we traveled the streets. Armed men in uniform were seen everywhere.

There were several physicians from other countries who had also been invited to present papers at the meeting. Dr. Kaplan and his wife Masha were from Israel; Dr. Jerry Glanz, one of Kaplan's students and his wife Joyce came from the United States; and Dr. John Carruth, a fine surgeon and expert on a special laser procedure known as *photo dynamic therapy*, practiced in Britain.

The entire foreign contingent was invited to go sightseeing the day after the completion of the conference. We had to get up at about 4:00 a.m. to begin what turned out to be an extremely long day of adventure. We rode in a utility vehicle with non-existent shock absorbers on a badly worn road. It was a long bumpy ride.

John Carruth had a particularly bad time of it. On the previous day, the visiting-speakers group had gone to lunch on the yacht of a real-estate tycoon. John went swimming off the stern of the boat in the Paraguay River. Not a good idea! He got sick and was feeling awful. To exacerbate matters he was assigned the worst seat on the vehicle, a folding-lawn chair. He was clearly miserable but a stalwart fellow.

The scenery was beautiful and impressive. We visited the Igwazu Falls, which are deep in a dense rain forest. Igwazu is not as high as, but is five times the width of, Niagara Falls and is much more spectacular because of its setting.

We toured the Itaipu hydroelectric power plant, which had the largest hydroelectric generating capacity in the world. At that time it was considered by some to be one of the seven wonders of the modern world. Itaipu is located at the corners where Brazil, Argentina and Paraguay meet. It supplies 75 percent of all the electric power utilized by the country of Paraguay and 25 percent of the electric power needs of Brazil.

On the return trip, our utility vehicle developed a flat tire. The spare tire was in poor shape, we were in the middle of nowhere, and it was already after dark. When we finally returned to our hotel it was perhaps nine in the evening. We were all very tired and worn out. We were told that there was a dinner scheduled for about ten o'clock; they have very late meals in South America.

I knew that if we went to the dinner, we would not be back in our hotel room until after midnight. Our flight to Argentina was set for eight the next morning.

Kathleen and I declined dinner and sent our apologies back with our associates. Our hosts took pity on us and changed our flight to eleven in the morning. The rest of the group attended the dinner and were there informed of the changed flight plan. Our fellow guests requested that Kathleen and I be advised of the changed flight plan and our hosts assured them that we had been informed.

But we had *not* been apprised of the changed plans! We didn't find out about the new flight plans until John Carruth passed our hotel room on the way to his room at about 1:00 a.m. and slipped our new tickets under our door. It would appear that we were being punished for not coming to dinner.

In the morning, we were glared at. Apparently, as happened on the previous three nights, we were scheduled to meet various Paraguayan dignitaries, but, for me, enough was enough.

**Terror in Argentina**

When we arrived in Argentina, I was informed that I was scheduled for another lecture tour. Again there had been no previous word about it.

One pleasant surprise was a ceremony at the University of Cordoba, one of the oldest Universities in the Americas. I received an honorary doctorate from the University and the ceremony was televised on Argentina national television.

The next day was long and hot. The city of Cordoba was in the midst of a heat wave and the transportation had no air-conditioning. The day's itinerary included a visit to the office of, and a meeting with, the Mayor of Cordoba as well as two more unscheduled lectures for me.

That night, Kathleen and I dressed to go to a dinner party at our host's home in Cordoba. Dr. Juri called the hotel and paged me in the lobby where we were waiting to be picked up for the party. He said: "You have had a long hot day, why don't you just relax and have dinner with your wife at the hotel? No need to come to the party." I said that it would be no trouble to attend since we were dressed for the party.

We had already gotten into enough trouble in Paraguay for missing a dinner! He was persistent and asked to speak with Kathleen.

This was very unusual. In South America, the husband usually has the last word. Juri implored Kathleen to stay away from the party and stated, "At least if you come, come casual." What was going on?

Unfortunately we did go. It was a very elaborate lawn party arranged around a large swimming pool with tables and torch lights and a very elegant buffet. I was the only man at the party without a tie, as per our host's wishes.

We were enjoying dinner and conversation with other guests when two loud gunshots disrupted the party atmosphere.

I thought that the shots had come from outside, but the next thing I knew, people were shouting and screaming. I saw John Carruth on the ground, stretched out. He yelled, "Get down!"[87]

Then, I looked around and saw six armed men in the party area. They were dressed in black slacks and red tee shirts. They carried rifles and pistols; at least one was armed with a semi-automatic weapon. They were terrorists and were barking orders to everyone present.

Between the din and the fact that they were speaking in Spanish, I couldn't begin to fathom what the terrorists were saying. I found out later that they had asked for me, by name, apparently with the intent to kidnap me. Someone had covered and told them that I didn't come to the party.

One of the women guests grabbed Kathleen, put her hand over Kathleen's mouth and moved her away from me. She was trying to keep Kathleen from also being kidnapped. I have never, ever, seen such a look of terror on anyone's face as I saw on that woman holding Kathleen.

Israeli surgeon, Isaac Kaplan, who had survived six wars in Israel, muttered, "Let's take them. There are only six of them and, more than fifty of us!" His wife Masha told him to be quiet.

We were herded, single file, past a table where every one, at gunpoint, was physically searched and ordered to empty wallets and give up all jewelry. Kathleen gave up her wedding ring, watch and earrings; I gave up a watch and wallet. This was turning out to be a very expensive trip!

---

[87] After sharing and surviving the South America adventure together, Dr. John Carruth, Kathleen and I became good friends. And, in 1994, John successfully nominated me for honorary inclusion in the Royal College of Surgeons of England.

Next we were herded in to a small room to await more action on the part of the terrorists. The rumor was that a strip search would be made but it didn't happen.

The terrorists then took their loot and disappeared into the night. Apparently neighbors called the police, but when they finally arrived, they were too late to do anything.

Most of us were in shock. After the terrorists departed, our host, Dr. Juri, admitted to me that earlier in the day the Mayor had offered police protection for the party. Juri refused, feeling we wouldn't need protection in Cordoba. *Then why did the Mayor offer it?*

Hugo told me that he still expected me to attend a scheduled ten o'clock meeting with the Governor of the Province the following morning. I said I wasn't interested.

"But, you have to," he remonstrated.

"No, I don't." I retorted.

There were some puzzling aspects to the "terrorist attack." The hostess continued to wear her earrings and other jewelry: when asked about it she said that they were paste. (You mean the terrorists recognized that fact?) The host had a wallet prominently in sight on the dining room table; it wasn't taken. There was a glass case with many valuables in plain sight in the dining room—none of them were touched.

Why were Kathleen and I called and told that we needn't attend the party? *We should have paid attention!*

At least, we had a police escort back to our hotel. Kathleen and I did not sleep all that night. In the morning we joined our host and the rest of the group for breakfast. I didn't hear any apologies for the terror of the night before. There was no "How are you?" or "Did you get any sleep?" No, the discussion was centered on the next International Society meeting scheduled for the following year in Buenos Aires, Argentina. The only concern was that the Americans would tell about the attack and there would then be a poor turnout for the Buenos Aires meeting and it would probably have to be moved to another location.

There was some good news: Kathleen and I were informed that we would not have to meet with the Governor of the Province. Canceled or not, there was no way that we were going to be at that meeting!

My only thought that morning was "We are leaving Argentina, *now*"! We didn't get much help from our host in this regard, but a police escort was provided not just to the airport, but also onto the aircraft itself. We left Argentina that same evening.

An explanation slowly emerged. We had visited Argentina at the height of the election campaign for the next President. The Governor of the Cordoba province was the front-runner and expected to be the winner by a large margin. News of our visit to Cordoba was published in a newspaper story and the credit for the visit was attributed to the Governor, who in turn was a close friend of Hugo Juri, our host. Apparently, the party that we attended was also announced and written up in the newspaper. An opposing candidate for president decided to discredit the Governor by raiding the party and abducting me.

Even though I wasn't actually kidnapped, the terrorist raid was written up in the newspapers and broadcast all over the country. The story appeared in newspapers all over South America and Mexico.

It worked. The Governor not only didn't become president, he was forced to resign. The Mayor of Cordoba resigned and the Police Chief was fired. Hugo Juri was ordered to appear in Buenos Aires and explain why he didn't have police protection at a party for foreign dignitaries.

The next meeting of the International Laser Society was held in Buenos Aires, after all.

EPILOGUE

# Afterthoughts

## Metamorphosis

As I look back, I think that I went through a metamorphosis of motivation in my career. Throughout, I was consistent in my intrigue with challenges to solve difficult problems. When I was studying for my doctorate at Stanford, my orientation was toward basic research. My thesis work was certainly challenging and I learned new technologies. I experienced a sense of satisfaction when I used creative ideas to solve some really difficult problems. But what did I actually accomplish? Although the measurement that I made was an important step in the basic understanding of science, what could I do with it? How could I explain the significance of the experiment and its' results to anyone except another physicist?

When I completed my work on the ruby maser, I could point with pride to the radical, creative new design that I had devised. It reduced the size and weight of the conventional maser configuration by a factor of 200 and simultaneously achieved a ten times improvement in performance. Yet, although this time I worked on something that could be touched and felt and I could see the results, in a sense it was a hollow victory. That maser still required cryogenic cooling and consequently was impractical.

*When the opportunity to work toward devising a laser afforded itself, the lights suddenly went on and the bells started ringing. The level of my excitement is hard to describe.*

Why?

Because this project had *everything*! There were the tough, challenging problems to solve that were severe enough, to give nagging doubts about whether the project could be accomplished at all. There was a feeling of fierce competition in the air. The subject matter was an area in which I was substantially prepared. I had the tools in place. Successful results would be of *breakthrough* scientific importance and yet at the same time, it had the real potential of something enormously useful.

I am reminded of an experienced actor who comes across a script that strikes a chord. *"I've got to have that part. That's the script I've been waiting for all my life."*

### It Should Have Been Done Earlier

Hundreds of different laser types have been demonstrated in the laboratory over the years. The laser has found many "homes" in a myriad of applications in countless, unconnected fields.

Given that so many lasers have been discovered, some scientists and journalists have engaged in philosophical mind-game writings. They argue "Look how *easy* it is to make a laser, it *should* have been done years earlier."

*It's great to have "20-20" hindsight; the presence effect.* The pre-laser period did foster many proposals, thoughts, ideas and concepts but nothing definitive. As repeatedly pointed out, a global effort was in place, but lasers were not forthcoming. Apparently, it was not so easy.

By 1960, the use of a ruby crystal for laser purposes had been abandoned and thoroughly discredited by respected and acclaimed scientists as well as all of the prominent laser teams (Bell, TRG, etc.). Researchers refused to work on ruby because it employed a ground-state lower laser level to operate, and the conventional wisdom was that only a "four-level" system with an elevated lower level was feasible.

If I hadn't persisted alone, out on a limb, it is quite clear that certainly in 1960, or soon thereafter, no one would have made a ruby laser. Think about it … *maybe never!* Having been discarded, there was not any drive to go back in that direction.

If laser-action in ruby had not been achieved, when would the first laser have come about?

In an attempt to answer that question, first consider and take into account the following: The announcement of the ruby laser achievement came as a huge shock that echoed through the scientific community. The excitement, inspiration and stimulus it provided for scientists both in and out of the field was incredible.

The doubts, which at this point were growing larger, were suddenly erased; *it actually could be done!* And the outpouring of new funding that resulted from that July 7, 1960 news announcement was enormous.

Since *crystal laser* development generally was spurred on and greatly accelerated by knowledge gained from the ruby device, it is unlikely that *any crystal* laser would have been realized for many years to come.

The gas laser of December 1960 was also unlikely to have been created without the ruby laser inspiration. Even before 1960, the gas laser attempts by Sanders at Bell Labs had already been abandoned. And, as verified by the twice previously cited *Bennett Science* magazine interview, Bell Labs was on the verge of cutting off Javan's funds. Bell only *reversed* direction and *increased* the funding and effort level for Javan's laser project *after* the ruby laser announcement.

Both the Columbia Radiation Laboratory and TRG were obsessed with alkali vapor systems. But these systems proved to be unworkable.[88]

In fact, there may not have been any lasers before the appearance of semiconductor lasers late in 1962! (Or later).[89]

The historical writers, who describe the creation of the laser as a race being "won by a hair", have been confused by the proliferation of lasers, which quickly followed the ruby. They seem to be oblivious to

---

[88] There was another kind of alkali-vapor infrared laser first conceived by Fabricant; later by a *one-sentence* treatment in the Schawlow-Townes paper; and mentioned by Gordon Gould in his "laundry list" of patent ideas. All of these proposals were devoid of any specific calculations or design data. The concept was to pump cesium (another alkali chemical element) with a helium discharge lamp. The Columbia group tried to make such a system, but was unsuccessful. TRG *alleged* to have succeeded with that infrared device in 1962. The reason I say *alleged*, is that in the *post* ruby period, from time to time, lasers would be reported which turned out to be "false alarms"—nobody could reproduce the results. Indeed, TRG quickly tore down their cesium apparatus and I'm not aware of any other laboratory that ever reproduced or verified the TRG data.

[89] Even the semiconductor laser's development timetable was moved forward and benefited from the success and inspiration of the ruby laser.

the explosive stimulus in research and funding level that immediately flowed as a result of the surprising ruby success story.

The ruby laser was, in fact, the fountain from which all other lasers grew. As noted before, it was the *king* of high-powered lasers for at least ten years.

Looking back, the reality is: the race was not won by a hair; it was won by a mile!

## Why Was I the One?

Why was I the one to make the first laser? ... Good question!

*I believe it was the result of full dedication, concentration, focus and tenacity ... Do not underestimate the intense drive and motivation of a maverick scientist.*

As I explained earlier, I never let go of the fact that I was working on something *that had never been done before.* I methodically and carefully traveled down the road toward the laser, one step at a time.

I avoided complicated devices and designs as well as impractical and cumbersome equipment including: vacuum systems, the complex processes in gas discharges, special mirror mechanisms and immature mirror coating technology. I also rejected corrosive chemical handling, cryogenics, new crystal growing programs and special lamp developments.

I pointedly stayed clear of a trend that a number of other scientists were ensnared into a phenomenon I describe as the "guru" effect. When established and acclaimed scientists set forth an agenda, there is a tendency for many disciples to, in effect, follow blindly.

When Schawlow and Townes set forth their potassium vapor proposal, few scientists questioned their calculations or the analysis of their proposal. (I may have been the only one). When Schawlow proclaimed the unworthiness of the pink ruby, again, his pronouncement was not questioned. The scientists who did follow those Schawlow-Townes principles were lead in unproductive directions.

I was adamant about keeping simplicity in my design approach and not getting sidetracked into special developments. In that regard I was successful, I ended up using commercially available ruby laser crystals, flashlamps and silver mirror coatings.

## Price War

All together, my laser development activity took nine and a half months from the start of a dedicated full time effort to its consummation.[90] It was a nerve-racking experience trying to counter-act the effects of all the negative conventional wisdom and the reluctant support. Although I was generally optimistic, I have to admit I certainly had my own doubts.

The entire project cost Hughes some $50,000 including salaries, equipment and all the overhead expenses. By contrast, TRG alone, consumed over one million dollars on their ARPA contract. And Ali Javan said that Bell Labs had put two million dollars into his gas laser project.[91] Hughes enjoyed one of the best research bargains of the era.

## Laser Nobel(s)

There have been seven Nobel prizes awarded to physicists as either a direct or indirect result of the laser. These include: Basov, Prokhorov and Townes, who basically worked out the theory and practice of the ammonia maser; Dennis Gabor, who worked out the theory of holography (three-dimensional photography); Kastler, who pioneered a particular concept of optical pumping (although different than that used in lasers); Arthur Schawlow for laser spectroscopy and Nicolas Bloembergen for non-linear optics.

The Nobel Foundation from time to time makes a mistake.[92] Since the foundation is private, it is beholden to no one. There are no checks and balances. The award for the *maser* may have been one of their errors.

I think it is fairly clear that the maser only came into enough prominence to warrant consideration by the Nobel physics committee *after* a laser existed and there was the alleged, but incorrect connection via the so called "optical maser." If the maser was really an important breakthrough, in and of itself, then it is more likely that prize would have been awarded much earlier; rather than 10 years after the maser came into existence. No, the maser prizes were not awarded until after there was a laser in existence.

---

[90] Of course, there was a lifetime of preparation behind those nine months including: the childhood electronics training in my father's home laboratory; the industrial job and laboratory experience; the long hours in the Stanford physics basement and guidance from Willis Lamb. (Maybe even that initiation from the light experiment in my mother's refrigerator was a factor).

[91] Previously cited Laser Pioneer Interviews, page 78.

[92] *It happens.*

There might be another factor in play. The Nobel committee responsible for the physics prize is the Swedish Royal Academy of Science. The committee is comprised entirely of academic members. They are, not surprisingly, highly biased toward academia. It is extremely rare that the Nobel physics committee awards prizes to non-academics. For example, Alexander Graham Bell (the telephone), Thomas Alva Edison (the electric light bulb) and the Wright Brothers (first manned flight) were never Nobel Laureates.

Even if the Nobel committee insisted on recognizing an academic person as per their pattern, I don't think they did their homework. It would have made more sense to recognize the Russian physicist Fabricant. Although, he didn't actually solve the laser problem, he thought of and proposed a laser before any of the work done by the maser scientists.

## Lasers in Medicine

From when I was a boy, continuing through my formative years, my father exerted strong pressures on me and attempted to shape my career. He tried to vicariously live again the way he would have liked to, if he could have started his career over again. He was particularly preoccupied with the idea that the then new field of electronics could be usefully employed to modernize and advance the archaic ways of medicine. He himself had experienced problems of acceptability and credibility, when he came up with new ideas to apply to make medical instrumentation more sophisticated. He was not a member of the "M.D. club."

His solution to the problem was for me to be trained in medicine as well as electronic engineering. I did try. I took a course in human physiology, at the Columbia University Medical School, in the summer between Stanford and my graduate physics work in the Columbia Physics Department. I didn't take to studies in the biological sciences very well—too much memorizing. I was more used to, and more comfortable with, the physical sciences since, by and large, they are very intuitive. I abandoned the medical direction and went on to my studies at Stanford as described earlier.

Yet, because of that educational experience, it is that much more important to me that such significant contributions to medicine are being made by the laser. Seeing and watching the development of revolutionary medical-laser procedures is especially gratifying and rewarding to me and it, happily fulfills my father's dream. His heart was in the right place.[93]

## A Concluding Thought

If anyone is creative and willing to entertain new and different concepts and pursue them, he or she might want to consider the following famous last words:

"Everything that can be invented has been invented."
Said in 1889 by Charles H. Duel, the director of the United States Patent Office.

"Heavier than air flying machines are impossible."
Said in 1895 by Lord Kelvin, President of the Royal Society.

"There is no likelihood man can ever tap the power of the atom."
Said in 1923 by Robert Millikin, the winner of a Nobel Prize in physics.

New ideas are destined to encounter negative reactions. Ignore the conventional wisdom.

## JUST, DO IT!

---

[93] It is even more heart warming that my father benefited from laser surgery on his eyes and my sister's vision is only now possible as a result of an available laser procedure. I myself was helped by a special laser procedure by Professor A. Hofstetter and Dr. R. Waidelich in Germany.

# INDEX